THE SOUL AT REST

BOOKS BY
TRICIA MCCARY RHODES

The Soul at Rest: A Journey Into Contemplative Prayer
Contemplating the Cross
Taking Up Your Cross

THE SOUL AT REST

TRICIA MCCARY RHODES

BETHANY HOUSE PUBLISHERS
MINNEAPOLIS, MINNESOTA 55438

Published by Bethany House Publishers
A Ministry of Bethany Fellowship International
11400 Hampshire Avenue South
Minneapolis, Minnesota 55438
www.bethanyhouse.com

Printed in the United States of America by
Bethany Press International, Minneapolis, Minnesota 55438

Library of Congress Cataloging-in-Publication Data

Rhodes, Tricia McCary.
    The soul at rest : a journey into contemplative prayer /
Tricia McCary Rhodes.
        p.   cm.
    ISBN 1–55661–809–3
    ISBN 0–7642–2227–9
    1. Prayer.   2. Contemplation.   3. Spiritual exercises.
4. Devotional calendars.   I. Title.
BV215.R46   1996
248.3'4—dc20   96–25279
                                                                              CIP

To Aunt Naomi,

who challenged me to fall in love with Jesus Christ,

and to my father,

who showed me how.

TRICIA McCARY RHODES is a freelance writer and worship coordinator for New Hope Church in San Diego, California. Her book flows from twenty-three years of full-time ministry and a longing to know Christ more deeply. Rhodes lives in California with her husband and has two children.

ACKNOWLEDGMENTS

I thank God, who is faithful to all generations, for the rich heritage of faith into which I was born. I know this is a rare gift. I am grateful for the people He has used in my life, especially as I wrote this book. To Richard Foster, whom I've never met, but who has mentored me through his writings: May you draw many more into the arms of our Savior. To Grandmother, who at ninety-two reminds me that God always has a purpose. To Mom, whose gentle support often sustains me. To my sisters, Carol and Susie, who have read, critiqued, and always believed the best for this project. To the staff and congregation of New Hope Church, who are living examples of His love; and to my friends, who read and gave me invaluable feedback: I am deeply indebted to each of you. To my husband and best friend, Joe: Thanks for always nudging me to follow God even if it meant sacrifice on your part. And also for months of dinners and dishes—I love you. To my sons, Champ and Jonathan, who bring me great joy: You are treasures. Finally, to Bethany House Publishers, and especially my editor, Steve Laube: Thanks for your passion for this subject and for having a vision that far exceeded my own.

CONTENTS

INTRODUCTION

Return to your rest, O my soul, for the Lord has dealt
bountifully with you.

Psalm 116:7

Weariness is written on our faces. We can't quite put our finger on it, but comments like, "I am so stressed out," and, "I'm so busy I don't know which end is up anymore," are heard every day. Always running, working, doing, learning, practicing, achieving, moving, climbing, pushing, thinking . . . we are plagued with a nagging feeling that something has been left undone.

Modern technology with the promise of a better life has thrown us into a tailspin. Constantly bombarded with high tech noise, we face choices so vast they overwhelm us. Our personal computers take us across the world in seconds, our televisions offer hundreds of channels, and even our cars have become offices from which we conduct the business of life over cellular phones. Yet, the unprecedented rate of change insists that we must run with the pack or be forever lost in the dusty dreams of simpler times.

Into all this commotion, God beckons, "Be still, and know that I am God" (Psalm 46:10, KJV). But can we hear Him? When we stop for a break, can we slow the pace of our minds enough to enjoy His gentle presence? Or is our faith just one more contribution to the cacophony of causes that demand our attention?

In truth, our only hope in this changing world is God who does not change. He is not taken off guard by the strides of science or the growth of technology. They are like clothes that wear out to Him. "Like clothing you will change them and they will be discarded. But you remain the same, and your years will never end" (Psalm 102:26–27, NIV).

This is God's perspective, but we struggle to internalize it. Many Christians long for a simpler faith—a deeper walk with God in the midst of the chaos we call life. Perhaps you do, too.

Are you:

- Hungry for a fresh touch from God?
- Weary of always running but never seeming to catch up?
- Well-equipped with knowledge about God but short on *knowing* Him?

Do you:

- Desire to slow down the pace of your busy life and be quiet in God's presence?
- Crave greater intimacy with God?
- Try to spend time in prayer but find yourself distracted or bored?
- Wish you could experience a new fervor in your pursuit of God?

If so, I want to invite you to join me on a life-changing journey in the presence of the living God. Today, this very moment, He bids you come and sit at His feet where you can experience reflection in place of restlessness, meditation instead of mindless activity, quiet in the midst of clamor, and waiting on Him rather than running about. This book calls you to the only kind of prayer that can create balance in the busyness of life.

Perhaps you aren't familiar with the term "contemplative prayer." It is an ancient term for a form of prayer that has been almost lost to the modern world. Very simply, contemplative prayer is communing with God through quiet moments of meditation, listening, and reflecting on Him. It is our response to God's call to "be still, and know."

This is called the "inner prayer journey" because instead of rushing into prayer with an agenda or grocery list of requests, we quiet our souls until God can speak and we are able to hear His gentle voice. His Word breathes new life into our spiritual walk as we let *Him* write its truths on our heart. We enter a love affair with the God of the universe.

My prayer is that this book will help you begin the journey and provide the tools needed to make contemplative prayer familiar and meaningful. As you peruse the pages and practice its truths, may you become the *soul at rest*.

CHAPTER ONE
THE JOURNEY BEGINS

Behold, now begins an eternal craving and insatiable longing.
Jan Van Ruysbroeck, A.D. 1293–1381

For each of us who follows Christ, there is a thirst within our soul that seeks to be quenched. We sense it in majestic moments of worship, or in rare instances of quiet prayer, as we taste the goodness of God's presence and long for more.

Maybe you have struggled, as I have, to capture these times with more consistency, to find fulfillment in your hunger to know God. For many years I read the Bible, prayed, and was committed to a life of obedience. But often, at the end of the day, I looked back with an emptiness borne of failure to hear God's voice or see His hand.

When reading of David, who longed for God "as the deer pants for the water brooks" (Psalm 42:1), I felt inadequate—ignorant of how to grasp that which seemed second nature to the psalmist. With diligence I pursued the disciplines I thought would make the difference. Yet, while change took place, an inner discontent remained. The more I *knew about God*, the more I wanted to *know Him*.

Augustine said, "You have made us for yourself, and our hearts are restless until they find their rest in You."[1]

But, how do we find this kind of rest? How do we satisfy the yearning within? Where is that "something more" that religious activity cannot provide? These were the burning questions in my heart.

In His faithfulness, God answered. Through the wisdom of believers who walked before me, I discovered how to be a child in His arms, a lamb in His protective embrace, and a lover hidden in the hollow of His heart. Jesus took my hand and we began a journey that will culminate in eternity when I see Him face-to-face.

Have you experienced this internal tug on your heart? Does something within want to "be taken into the arms of a God who will never forsake you from his embrace?"[2] To find some way of "resting in Him whom you have found, who loves you, who is near to you, and who comes to draw you to himself?"[3]

God wants to meet your deepest needs. He wants you to see, know, taste, and experience Him in ways that shake you to your core. He longs for you far more than you could ever long for Him. He stands ready to reveal himself, enfold you in love, speak to you with power, and touch you with grace. He has waited for you—for this moment. Are you ready?

Using This Book

As a little girl, I loved to play with my mother's sewing basket. It was filled with mysterious and wonderful things—a veritable treasure chest of tools to bring new life to the knees of worn-out jeans or create a doll of discarded rags. My son, the inventor, never loses interest in his father's toolbox—it is amazing what he can build with a hammer, screwdriver, and a few nails.

This book is not a how-to manual, but a package of tools to deepen your walk with God. Like the sewing basket or toolbox, you may use the contents to create and plot your own pilgrimage.

Each chapter is divided into five sections with an inspirational reading and a personal contemplative exercise. You will probably want to have a blank notebook handy for personal responses. The time you spend on each will vary as the Spirit leads. While each chapter stands alone, they are woven together in a tapestry of time-worn principles.

If your spiritual journey is just beginning, this book can help you to know and receive God's love. If you have traveled in His presence for some time, it can lead to deeper waters of faith. This is your journey, but you will not be alone. Truth from Scripture and testimony from the lives of saints throughout the ages will accompany you—the living God will guide you.

DAY ONE: A PASSION

The apostle Paul's dramatic conversion brought him face-to-face with the reality of a living God. Then he spent three years alone in the desert in a kind of spiritual training camp, with Jesus his only teacher. He traveled the rest of his days as an itinerant missionary, revolutionizing the scope of God's kingdom on earth.

Paul's passion for God could not be contained. *That I may know Him* was his heart's cry through the most vile and dangerous circumstances any believer ever faced (Philippians 3:8–10). After years of suffering, his heart overflowed with wonder at the God he had come to know. "Oh, the depth of the riches both of the wisdom and knowledge of God! How unsearchable are His judgments and unfathomable His ways!" (Romans 11:33).

What Is the One Thing?

Today, most of us are overwhelmed with our lives. We juggle careers, family responsibilities, civic duties, and community involvement. The needs around us are tyrants at our doors, and we long for even a moment of peace and quiet. But the dishes must be washed, the school needs volunteers, and the boss wants a few more hours on a project.

Money really doesn't grow on trees, and we never seem to have enough.

Feeling the weight of ministry, we take on the spiritual needs of our church. Whatever passion we may have had for God has gotten lost in the stresses of life as we catapult toward the next century. Are there any answers?

Jesus reminds us that though we may run ourselves ragged at times, like Martha, the one thing we must purpose to do is sit at His feet, like Mary (Luke 10:40–42). He issues an eternal invitation: "If any man is thirsty, let him come to Me and drink" (John 7:37). The promise is: "Open your mouth wide and I will fill it . . . with honey from the rock I would satisfy you" (Psalm 81:10, 16). It is so simple, we may miss it.

God wants us to be passionate about knowing Him. "And this is eternal life, that they may know Thee" (John 17:3). Jeremiah pronounced: "Thus says the LORD, 'Let not a wise man boast of his wisdom, and let not the mighty man boast of his might, let not a rich man boast of his riches; but let him who boasts boast of this, that he understands and knows Me'" (Jeremiah 9:23–24). Nothing else matters—not intellect, success, or the ability to influence others—just knowing Him. That's it.

What drew you to this book? Whatever need you sense is there for one reason—to cause you to come to the Father and sit at His feet. God is drawing you to himself. He wants to wrap His arms around you and fill you with a passion to know Him more.

Using a Prayer Journal

The inner prayer journey is an exciting one and can be chronicled through a prayer journal. I have found a spiral notebook works best. You will want to respond to what God shows you. Jot down the date and whatever is on your heart. This will be helpful as you return to it again and again to track your journey, to see God's hand, and to reflect on the treasures you have discovered.

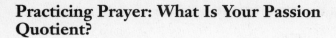

Practicing Prayer: What Is Your Passion Quotient?

Heart Preparation

Spend a few minutes to become quiet before God. Thank Him for His love and commitment to you. Ask for His guidance through this exercise.

Which of the following best describes your desire to know God right now?

- Something that burns within me
- Something that takes second place to so many other things
- Something I want, but don't seem to pursue
- Something that fluctuates depending on my circumstances
- Not really a desire but my duty as a Christian
- A gentle nudge I can't get away from
- Other

Below are several descriptions of God. Read at least one passage for each description. Which ones have you personally experienced in your relationship with God?

- Shepherd (Psalm 23; Luke 15:3–7)
- Father (Matthew 6:9; Luke 15:11–32)
- Friend (Proverbs 18:24; John 15:13–15)
- Lord (John 20:26–28; Romans 14:7–9)
- Sheltering wings (Ruth 2:12; Matthew 23:37)
- Comforting arms (Deuteronomy 33:27; Mark 10:14–16)

Write a prayer in your prayer journal telling God how you feel about the inner prayer journey and what you would like to receive from Him. Be honest, asking for His help where you are weak.

DAY TWO: THE TIME

A little discipline goes a long way when you are beginning to spend time with God. It is important to have a set time each day, and a consistent amount of time for prayer.

A Set Time

David, the psalmist, a man after God's own heart, sought God most often in the early morning hours.

> In the morning, O LORD, Thou wilt hear my voice; in the morning I will order my prayer to Thee and eagerly watch (Psalm 5:3).
> But I, O LORD, have cried out to Thee for help, and in the morning my prayer comes before Thee (Psalm 88:13).
> I rise before dawn and cry for help; I wait for Thy words (Psalm 119:147).

Isaiah, the prophet who encountered God's glory in the temple, records the Lord's words:

> The Lord GOD has given Me the tongue of disciples ... He awakens Me morning by morning, He awakens My ear to listen (Isaiah 50:4).

I prefer the early morning for several reasons. First, it provides a sense of God's presence and perspective with which to face the day. Second, when prayer is my first priority, other things cannot crowd it out. While I try to commune with God throughout the day, my waking moments are His alone. I want to hear from Jesus before I do anything else.

Another time may work better for you. Jesus went away in the night, the middle of the day, and the early morning hours to be alone with God. Find a time that works for you on a regular basis. Jesus emphasized consistent daily prayer when he taught the disciples to pray: "Give us this day our *daily* bread" (Matthew 6:11, emphasis added).

Something about our nature adapts to consistency. If you change the time a lot, you will probably have more difficulty establishing a pattern of daily prayer. But, do not be rigid. If you miss your planned time for some reason, God doesn't abandon you. Come to Him later, or seek Him the next day.

A Reasonable Goal

The length of time depends on your current walk with God. If you have been having quiet times for years, you might be ready for an hour or even two each day. If this is something new or you have struggled to be disciplined in this area, set a reasonable goal.

I believe that even ten minutes set aside *every* day brings greater growth and desire for God than sporadic times throughout the week. But remember, this is *your* spiritual journey—no one else's. God looks at the heart and is touched by your desire to be with Him.

Practicing Prayer: Time Out to Think About Time

Heart Preparation

Become still and quiet in God's presence. Ask Him to speak in love, drawing you to himself through these questions.

How much time have you spent daily in the past several weeks getting to know God in prayer?

How much time would you like to be able to spend?

What are the things that keep you from spending as much time as you would like?

What was David's perspective on time management? (See Psalm 39:4–7; 90:10–12.)

How might this perspective help in planning for your quiet time?

What would be a realistic amount of time to commit to spending with God on a daily basis?

What is the best time of day for you to be alone with God?

What will be the hindrances to this time?

What can you do to minimize these distractions?

DAY THREE: THE PLACE

Does it matter where we decide to spend time with God? While God is not limited to any location, *we* need structure. Jesus affirmed this when he taught His disciples about prayer. "But you, when you pray, go into your inner room, and when you have shut your door, pray to your Father who is in secret, and your Father who sees in secret will repay you" (Matthew 6:6). This passage reveals some helpful hints.

Three Things

1. *A place prepared for prayer.* Some families decorate their guest room for private devotions, others have a small altar—a table with an open Bible— which beckons them. Your circumstances may not allow such extravagance, but we can all find some way to get away. (I remember my father shutting himself in the bathroom—the only room in the house with a lock—in order to escape the cries of five young children and be alone with God.)

My place is the corner of my living room. This room stays fairly neat, so I don't get as distracted by things to do. A basket, filled with all the things I need in my time alone with God stays there. I have a portable cassette player for music, and a soft lamp for atmosphere. On winter days, the fireplace adds warmth and ambiance. With coffee in hand, I anticipate a special time with my friend—the Lord.

A Quiet Time Basket/Box

Create your own basket or box to enhance your quiet time. There are several things to include.
- *Your favorite Bible, plus another translation*
- *A journal for thoughts and prayers (a blank notebook works great)*
- *A blank notebook for Scripture meditations*
- *A devotional guide or book on prayer*
- *3×5 notecards for meditative thoughts or verses*
- *Stationery for writing to those God brings to mind in prayer*

---

2. *A secluded place.* Ideally, this should be a place where you shut out distractions. I can do this in my living room because I rise earlier than the rest of my family. (By the way, when my young son interrupts me, I let him lay quietly on the couch while I sing or pray. Rubbing his back or stroking his hair, I consider God's love for me—his needy child.)

Turn off the telephone, the television, the radio, and all the other things that nag you to get busy. Jesus tells us to *shut the door.* By doing this, we affirm we want to be alone with Him; nothing else matters for these few minutes.

There are other special places for time with God. Nature is a wonderful way to see the handiwork of God and be led into His presence, whether walking in the wintry woods or basking in the sea's balmy breezes. While few of us live in a place where we can do this daily, we can make special plans to meet God, just as we might a rendezvous with the one we love.

3. *An inner room.* Teresa of Avila, a woman of God from the sixteenth century, wrote a book depicting our hearts as castles with many rooms in which God seeks to dwell and fill with His presence. In the center is a room where the soul unites with God. This is the room we aspire to dwell in as often as we can.

> Once you get used to enjoying this castle, you will find rest in all
> things, even those involving much labor, for you will have the hope
> of returning to the castle, which no one can take from you.[4]

This is the room of the heart—the soul, our interior being. Catherine of Siena, a fourteenth-century believer who devoted her life to prayer calls us to the inner room this way: "Build yourself a cell in your heart and retire there to pray."[5]

Thomas Kelly describes it as an "amazing, deep inner sanctuary of the soul to which we may continuously return."[6]

The inner prayer journey explores this place within where God's Spirit dwells.

This may seem a little mysterious for now, but it will become clearer as we go along. Jesus taught that His kingdom is within us. Our bodies house the Spirit of the living God. As we learn to use the tools He has provided, we will discover more of His ways and thoughts, enabling us to visit often this inner place of refuge and rest.

Wandering Thoughts

What do I do when my mind won't stay focused?

- *Don't fight mental distractions or try to resist—this will make it worse!*
  (What happens when I say: Don't think about a pink elephant?)
- *Do jot down things to do later on a piece of paper.*
- *Do picture yourself filing thoughts in an imaginary file cabinet for future perusal.*
- *Do write your anxieties, emotions, fears, in a journal.*
- *Do see distracting thoughts flowing by you in a stream, emptying into the vast ocean's waves.*
- *Do gently return to prayer when you have released them.*
- *Don't let them get you down—every thought you have is known first by God.*
- *Do keep on trying—it will get easier with practice!*

Practicing Prayer: There's a Place for You

Heart Preparation

Take some time to be aware of God's presence. Thank Him for all He has done in your life this week. Ask Him to shine His light as you consider these questions.

What place in your house (or elsewhere) would be best to use consistently for your quiet time?

What can you do to make it special and/or ready for your time with God?

What are some other special places you could visit for an extended time alone with God?

Read Acts 7:48–50. What does God say about location concerning His presence?

Where does God dwell according to Ephesians 3:14–19?

Read 1 Corinthians 3:16. What does it mean to be a "temple of God"?

What does the concept of an *inner room* mean to you?

What are some things you might do to begin to build an altar within?

DAY FOUR: THE PLAN

While we will learn and use different tools on our journey, purposeful preparation can enhance their effectiveness. Three habits help us ready our hearts and minds for a meaningful time of prayer.

Anticipate

As a child, I cherished the times when my grandparents came to visit. The days couldn't pass fast enough until they arrived. Thoughts of what they would bring, and the wonderful times we would have filled my waking moments and dream-filled sleep.

This is the kind of expectancy we can have every day on a spiritual level. God, our heavenly Father, loving Counselor, peace-giving Friend, and gentle Shepherd is coming to see us. His arms are laden with gifts that will change our lives. Let the thought of this fill your day.

"It is the Lord's voice speaking, calling us to Him, yet sometimes so quietly at first that without stopping to listen, we don't hear it. But the call is real. The Lord is there."[7]

The Lord is there—what a mind-boggling thought. The Almighty God, Creator of the universe, has come to spend time with you. You are the recipient of His undivided attention. He has a plan—the blueprint of your life—written in the palm of His hand. Remind yourself before going to bed at night—the Lord is here!

Acknowledge

As you begin your devotional time, acknowledge that God is present. It may be helpful to say something like: *I come to be with you this morning, Lord. Thank you for your faithfulness and constant presence with me. Thank you for taking time to spend with me. I offer myself to you for this important interval together.* We may not feel God's presence, but He is always with us; affirming this verbally increases our awareness.

Sometimes I come as a child, ready to sit at His feet, His hand on my head. Other times I am the prodigal son, plodding down the road, taken aback by His eager arms and running feet. I might tell Him of my condition as a lost lamb, needy and afraid, longing to rest in His arms. There are many ways to acknowledge the presence of God.

For some, it helps to imagine Jesus sitting in a chair nearby, ready to speak and listen. His presence is as real as the chair in front of us. If nothing else happens except that we know He is here, our lives will change. Take time to acknowledge God's commitment to meet you in your place of prayer.

Acclimate

It is not easy for most of us to be quiet before God. Our minds race, our bodies resist, and we feel like we're wasting our time. But there are things we can do to create a quiet heart.

First, be comfortable, but not too comfortable. In Scripture, people bowed, stood, lay down, sat, or knelt when praying. We want to be in a posture that requires little thought. (Kneeling always makes my feet fall asleep!) Many find sitting in a chair with both feet on the floor best. Richard

Foster, well-known author on the subject of prayer, suggests we place our palms up on our knees to symbolize a heart of receptivity and expectation.[8]

The important thing is to be relaxed and free from distractions.

Second, close your eyes and slow the pace of your mind. Take deep breaths, concentrating on relaxing your body. Establish a slow, rhythmic pattern. Breathe in God's peace, and breathe out your stresses, distractions, and fears. Breathe in God's love, forgiveness, and compassion, and breathe out your sins, failures, and frustrations.

Make every effort to "stop the flow of talking going on within you—to slow it down until it comes to a halt."[10]

Don't work too hard at this—be patient with yourself. It will get easier with practice. Our Western world has not prepared us to hear the still, small voice of God breaking through our busyness. We must train ourselves to do so.

Many people find it helpful to play quiet instrumental music at the beginning of their devotional time. Discover what helps you become acclimated to the recreating quiet of God's presence. Through practice, it will come quickly and feel more natural.

❧ ❧

Holy Drowsiness

Many people feel guilty when prayer lulls them to sleep. Some ancient contemplatives felt this to be a special place in the heart of God. Francis of Sales said, "I had rather be asleep on the breast of God than awake in any other place." Teresa of Avila called it holy drowsiness *and encouraged us not to feel defeated. Try to be well rested when praying, but if you fall asleep, remember you are in God's arms, loving Him—you have not failed.*[9]

Practicing Prayer: What's Your Plan?

Heart Preparation

Spend a few minutes placing your trust in God's hands. Acknowledge His presence during this time. Thank Him for His supernatural plan for your life.

In Psalm 16:7–8, how did David anticipate God's presence? When?

In what ways can you establish the habit of *anticipating* God's presence in your quiet time? Throughout the day? At night?

Read Deuteronomy 31:8 and Matthew 28:20. What promise can you claim for your quiet time?

Write in your prayer journal what you might say to God to *acknowledge* His presence during your time alone with Him.

What things make it difficult for you to become quiet in God's presence? How can you plan to deal with these ahead of time?

Thank God right now for His commitment to you. Acknowledge His presence right here and now. Close your eyes and take a few deep breaths. Open your eyes, but continue breathing as follows:

Inhale as you say, *Lord Jesus, I receive Your love.*

Exhale as you say, *I release guilt and fear.*

Inhale as you say, Lord Jesus, *I receive Your truth*.

Exhale as you say, *I release anxiety and distrust.*

Inhale as you say, Lord Jesus, *I receive Your peace.*

Exhale as you say, *I release tension and fretfulness.*

Inhale as you say, Lord Jesus, *I receive Your light.*

Exhale as you say, *I release my sin and disobedience.*

Did you find yourself relaxing? Practice this in the coming days.

DAY FIVE: THE COMMITMENT

Does the idea of meeting God every day bring anticipation and longing to your heart? Is it worth sacrificing the time and energy out of your already busy schedule? If so, it is time to prayerfully consider making a specific commitment. The Creator is calling you to venture into the river of life. You may only go ankle deep at first, but you will learn to enjoy the cool depths of this life-giving source.

Remember, no one else will walk the road you walk—it is yours alone. But you will be holding the hand of the Good Shepherd who has promised to lead you beside still waters, give you rest in green pastures, and restore your soul. What could be more encouraging?

The following thoughts are designed to help you make this commitment to yourself and God concerning your future devotional life. It is not a ruler for anyone else to measure your spirituality by, or for you to beat yourself over the head with, but a secret covenant of the heart between you and the Lover of your soul. He stands with hands outstretched. Will you come along?

Practicing Prayer: At Water's Edge

Heart Preparation

Spend a few minutes reviewing your responses to the issues of passion, place, time, and plan. (Don't skip this—it is crucial to your decision.) Based on these, ask God for guidance and grace as you consider making a commitment to Him.

Give Him time to reveal anything that might hinder your relationship with Him right now. Confess your complete dependency on Him.

When you are ready, write a prayer of commitment. This should reflect the desires of your own heart concerning the inner prayer journey. You may write your own or use the one below for your prayer journal.

Jesus: I want to know You more. Please take my desire and make it a burning passion. By Your grace and through Your power alone, I commit to spending _____ (amount of time) with You every day that I can. I will usually be doing this at _____ (time of day). The place I will meet You is _____ (location). Though You are always present with me, I believe You will meet me in a special way during these times together. I plan to begin this journey of inner prayer on _____ (date and time). I need You to enable me to follow through by the power of Your Spirit who lives in me. Your child and follower:

Signed _____ *Date*_____

Read this prayer aloud two or three times over the next few days, before beginning the next chapter, to crystallize your commitment. Don't become rigid or legalistic—that may cause frustration and could drive you away from God. If you fail, remember your heavenly Father is not surprised or dismayed. He doesn't want to punish or coerce you into submission. He is delighted with every effort you make. You are His child. He is there to pick you up, give wisdom, and help you move forward once again.

Moving Forward

The purpose of this chapter has been to provide some form and structure for your inner prayer journey. You will decide how to fill it in. The rest of the book opens up many options. Don't rush any part of it—some will take longer than others.

❧ ☙

Enhancing Your Quiet Time

There are some simple things to enhance your quiet time as you move forward. A few are listed below. Add to this list as you grow in the grace of knowing God.

- *Read aloud from the Psalms, personalizing the verses.*
- *Sing a few praise choruses or well-known hymns.*
- *Listen to a quiet worship tape or CD.*
- *Speak aloud all that you are thankful for this day.*
- *Praise God for the beauty of His creation in specific ways.*
- *Read the words of Christ from the Gospels.*
- *Read from a daily devotional book.*
- *Read a section from a book on prayer.*

Would you like to live your life always aware of God's perspective instead of being controlled by circumstances? In the next chapter we will learn how our minds can become storehouses of spiritual strength and truth, releasing peace and freedom within. Getting God's perspective and seeing it permeate your soul through Meditative Prayer will radically change the way you live.

Notes

1. Augustine of Hippo, *Augustine's Confessions* (Grand Rapids, Mich.: Sovereign Grace Publishers, 1971), p. 1.
2. Eddie Ensley, *Prayer That Heals Our Emotions* (San Francisco: Harper and Row, 1988), p. 5.
3. Thomas Merton, *Contemplative Prayer* (New York: Herder and Herder, 1969), p. 39.
4. Teresa of Avila, *The Interior Castle*, as quoted in Richard Foster, *Devotional Classics* (New York: HarperCollins, 1993), p. 199.
5. Catherine of Siena, as quoted in Jill Haak Adels, *The Wisdom of the Saints* (New York: Oxford University Press, 1987), p. 41.
6. Thomas R. Kelly, *A Testament of Devotion* (New York: Harper and Row, 1941), p. 35.
7. Emilie Griffin, *Clinging, the Experience of Prayer* (San Francisco: Harper and Row, 1984), p. 11.
8. Foster, p. 24.
9. Ensley, p. 34.
10. Morton T. Kelsey, *The Other Side of Silence* (New York: Paulist Press, 1976), p. 103.

CHAPTER TWO

MEDITATIVE PRAYER

There is a place within where the sea is always calm and the boats are steady, and Christian meditation takes our awareness to that place.
Eddie Ensley

Imagine waking up one morning to a piercing silence—no radio, TV, or traffic. You wander around for hours, accompanied only by the sounds of nature and the warmth of the sun on your face. Night falls. With nothing but time on your hands, you lay on your back gazing at the galaxy of stars brightening the dark sky.

This was the lifestyle for a shepherd boy named David who was called in from the hills to be made king over Israel. He was an unlikely candidate, yet God chose him above many others. The reason: David was *a man after God's own heart* (1 Samuel 13:14). Wouldn't you love to have God say that about you?

How did David acquire such a lofty label? Perhaps those hundreds of hours alone on the hillsides had drawn him in intimacy to the God of his father. Through days of praise and nights of meditation, David could say from personal experience, "The LORD is my shepherd, I shall not want" (Psalm 23:1).

Meditation is the first step on our inner prayer journey because it lays the groundwork for deep and searching communion with God. Through it, we allow God to speak, and to create conditions that enable us to hear and to respond.

Have you heard the voice of God lately? God is always revealing himself, yet how often we miss what He is saying because our busy world keeps us from cultivating the soil of our hearts. We are pilgrims on a journey, passing through a foreign land. Struggle is inevitable; we get hurt and broken. Plus we are bombarded daily with the values of this world.

It is tough to hear the voice of God in the midst of a clamoring culture. Yet God invites us to see each day as He sees it, in light of eternity. Through Meditative Prayer our minds and hearts are able to comprehend and internalize truth. When we do, we are changed.

◄ ►

Just a Note

While these chapters are divided into days, this is simply a guideline. You may not have time to do the reading and the exercises in one day's devotional time. Feel free to spend several days on one section as necessary.

DAY ONE: THE COMPONENTS

The inner prayer journey calls us to encounter the Redeemer who has purchased us with His own blood and come to live within us through His Spirit. In Meditative Prayer, the mind, heart, and will unite. A focus on one without the others will fall short of deepening our relationship with Christ.

Meditative Prayer and the Mind

Star-gazing. I love to look at the dark tapestry of night with its lights scattered like grains of sand across black paper. I'm a novice—not good at spotting things like the Big Dipper or the Milky Way. If I were an astronomer, I could observe planets and comets, satellites or meteors, galaxies and clusters of galaxies. Through the eye of my telescope the night sky would come to life.

What does this have to do with meditation? We are spiritual astronomers. At first glance, we see the broad scope of truth like the tapestry of stars on the night sky. But as we allow God to focus the telescope of our minds, we move in closer, gaining precision as we go. Then we explore until truth penetrates our vision.

Recently I was meditating on Colossians 3:1: "If then you have been raised up with Christ, keep seeking the things above, where Christ is, seated at the right hand of God." First, I contemplated what the "things above" might be. Then I consulted the cross-reference in my Bible and read several related verses concerning "earthly things." One verse talked about gratifying selfish desires, another was Jesus' response when Peter objected to His imminent death. "You are not setting your mind on God's interests, but man's" (Matthew 16:23). A clear picture began to form in my mind of that which keeps me from focusing on "things above."

Is There a Wrong Way to Meditate?

The meditation taught in Scripture differs greatly from that of Eastern religions. It is important to understand the differences.

Christian Meditation	*Eastern Meditation*
Focuses on filling the mind with an awareness of God's presence.	*Focuses on emptying the mind.*
Recognizes Holy Scripture as the only standard by which truth is established.	*Recognizes no objective reference for establishing truth.*

Encourages one to understand and identify God's reality.	*Encourages one to withdraw from reality.*
Highest level is an encounter with the living God.	*Highest level is "nirvana"—a complete merging of one's self into the consciousness of the universe.*
Dependent upon the indwelling Holy Spirit to accomplish God's purposes within us.	*Dependent upon one's human ability to achieve a certain state.*
Results in a gaining of our true identity in Christ.	*Results in a loss of personal identity.*
Has as its goal greater love for God and service to others.	*No goal outside of the experience itself.*

Beginning with Scripture is one way. (We'll come back to this later.) Another is to choose a theme and then gather information. Read related Scripture, recall God's hand in your own life, the testimonies of others, the truths found in nature or other sources. (You will discover specific ways to do this in the next four days.)

A friend once came to me concerned about her spiritual life. She was a Bible student at heart, having participated in and taught studies for fifteen years. She could explain complex issues from Genesis to Revelation. But her words reflected great discouragement: "I don't know how to just *be* with God. How can I get to know Him?"

It's a common struggle. Many committed Christians' lives confirm the reality that discovering truth is not in itself enough to change us or draw us into God's loving embrace. Only as knowledge moves from our head to our heart, will we experience the fullness of joy found in God's presence.

Meditative Prayer and the Heart

Andrew Murray, known by his passion for prayer, says that with our minds we gather and prepare spiritual food to eat.[1]

In order to move to the heart, we feed on this spiritual food—tasting, chewing, and digesting. Our hearts are nourished and our souls satisfied. This is the core of Meditative Prayer and we should occupy most of our time in it.

During my meditation on Colossians 3:1, I reviewed my notes from the related verses. At first I was overwhelmed. I felt like the things of earth were in my heart and thoughts far more than things above. But as I prayed, the words "keep seeking" caught my attention. I let them roll through my mind and heart several times.

"Keep seeking . . . keep seeking . . . keep seeking." After a while, I felt a sense of rest, as if God were telling me my responsibility was just to *keep seeking* and not to focus on the results. He reminded me that while my life still contained much that was not of Him, He was changing me—I only had to keep looking to Him. Peace and fresh motivation settled within.

This is the kind of truth we want to hold close. Letting our minds rest, our hearts become still and quiet, allowing the sense of God's presence to saturate our soul. Do not rush this time but wait on God to complete His work. Let Him captivate you with His love.

It isn't always easy, but through practice this becomes a valuable source of spiritual growth.

> The reward of resting for a time from intellectual effort, and cultivating the habit of holy meditation, will come in the course of time. The two will be brought into harmony and all our study will be animated by quiet waiting on God and the yielding of the heart and life to the Word.[2]

Meditative Prayer and the Will

When you sense God has spoken and you have experienced His presence, you will be drawn to respond. Contemplate what difference this encounter might make in your life. Ask God to accomplish what He wants; confess past sin, pray for grace and strength, commit to sharing this with a friend or anything God may lead you to do.

As part of my Colossians 3:1 meditation, I thanked God that I was in a process of change; He didn't demand perfection at once. I expressed my longing to be a person whose mind was continually set on Him, asking forgiveness for a recent outburst of anger and my love of material things. I committed to regular times of meditation on the fruit of the Spirit.

This is Meditative Prayer—an exercise that begins with our minds, permeates our hearts, and finds fruition in acts of obedience. We have brought every part of our self to this experience and heard the voice of God. We know Him more and perhaps understand a little better our true identity as His child.

🖎 🖎

Meditating Made Easy—Mind-Heart-Will

Mind *Look at the broad scope.*
What truths are seen here?
Look up related verses.
Narrow your subject.
What is the most important part of this truth for me today?
Tune in to truth until you see clearly.

Heart *Look more intently.*
Lord, what are you saying to me?
When truth touches your heart, stop and wait on Him.
Spend the most time here.

Will *Make a decision, a commitment, or confession.*
How will your life change because of this?
End with praise and worship.

Practicing Prayer: Freedom

Heart Preparation

Take time to *Acclimate*. (Review that section in Chapter 1, if you need to.) Affirm the presence of the Holy Spirit. Ask God to teach you from His heart today.

The Mind: Read Romans 8:15–16 silently. Now read the passage again aloud, personalizing it (*For I have not received. . . .*)

Think about these questions:

To what were we once slaves?

Who has adopted us?

How can we know this for sure?

Why are we free from fear?

(Look up cross-references on this passage. Write down pertinent thoughts in your prayer journal.)

Narrow it down. Choose one of these words to ponder: Slavery . . . Fear . . . Adoption . . . Spirit . . . Abba.

Ask:

What does it mean?

Why should I understand it?

What is God saying about it?

(Again, write down significant thoughts.)

The Heart: Mentally release distracting thoughts as you personalize this aspect of your relationship with God.

Ask:

What do you want me to know Lord?

What are you saying?

Who am I and who are you in light of this?

You will know when God has spoken. Treasure this thought. Turn it over and over in your heart and mind. Experience the truth of it. Rest in it. Do not rush.

Pour out your response to God. Worship Him in the quietness of this moment.

The Will: Seek God's will concerning this.

Ask:

What do You want me to do?

How do You see me changing?

How can I live this truth you have given?

Write your response in your prayer journal.

Commit to memorizing this passage or reading it daily for one week.

DAY TWO: WHAT GOD HAS TO SAY

Abraham gazed at the stars to comprehend God's plan, Job explored the forces of nature to understand God's character and the prophet Jeremiah meditated on the potter and clay to seek God's will.

While most specific biblical references to meditation come from the life of David as poured out in the Psalms, God's people often demonstrated Meditative Prayer. From them we learn that Meditative Prayer's benefits are bountiful, and its purpose profound.

Meditative Prayer's Bountiful Benefits

When I was a child, we camped by a clear blue lake in northern California every summer. A highlight of the trip was swinging on the tire that hung from the large oak tree and dropping into the water. The tree's branches spread halfway into the lake; there were a dozen places to hide within its bushy foliage. Year after year, every day of summer, children from two to sixty-two climbed its sturdy trunk for the thrill of the swing.

That tree took a lot of abuse. Yet it was a grand sight, and each year as our old station wagon pulled to a stop in front of the rugged campground, I flew from the car to see if it was still there. I was never disappointed. Far down the winding dirt trail I could see that tree regally standing, barely swaying in the breeze.

We can be like that. The Bible teaches that as we make meditation the habit of our life, we will stand firm, battered but not destroyed by the abuses this world brings. Year after year, we will see fresh growth springing from within. We will experience deep spiritual thirst, but always be quenched, because like the tree we are planted by streams of living water. (Psalm 1:3)

God stands before you holding a treasure chest of meditation's precious jewels. He invites you to make it your own. If you were to open it and look inside, you would find it holds:

- A heart's desire to do God's will
- An overflow of your spiritual life into the lives of others
- Wisdom to make every decision you face (Joshua 1:8).

The benefits of meditation are truly bountiful, almost too good to be true. How different things would be if we experienced even a portion of what God offers. These promises alone are enough to compel us to meditate. Yet, God holds out something far greater.

Meditative Prayer's Profound Purpose

What would make a man like David cry from the depths of his heart: "One thing I have asked from the LORD, that I shall seek . . . to behold the beauty of the LORD, and to meditate in His temple"? (Psalm 27:4). These words reflect a passion born of far more than wanting a return on his spiritual investment.

David understood the secret that meditation offered "nothing less than a fiery and eternal love affair with the passionate and all-compassionate Lover who dances throughout the cosmos and in the bosom of our own hearts."[3]

Meditative Prayer's highest calling is an encounter with the King of kings who knocks at our heart's door, longing to commune with us. This is profound.

Does your heart long for this kind of intimacy? Are you tired of dryness and spiritual impotency? Has your mind been saturated with truth, yet your heart unmoved? Through Meditative Prayer, God will break through the barriers and flood your life with water from the well that never runs dry.

Practicing Prayer: Where Can I Flee From Your Presence?

Heart Preparation

Take the time to *acknowledge* God's presence and *acclimate* yourself to it. Ask the Holy Spirit to be your guide today. Yield your mind, heart, and will to His purposes.

The Mind: Read Psalm 139:1–18 aloud slowly, as if you had just written it yourself. Read verses 7–12 aloud one more time, making it a personal prayer.

Ponder the following questions in light of the passage:

What makes me want to run from You sometimes, Lord?

What things frighten me most about my life?

What can I count on in my relationship to You?

How close are You really?

Can I ever flee from Your presence?

When I feel mostly darkness and can't see what You are doing in my life, where are You then?

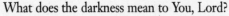

What does the darkness mean to You, Lord?

Write down your thoughts in your prayer journal.

The Heart: Read verses 7–12 one more time aloud. Take a few minutes to let the words sink in.

Ask God:

Where can I flee from Your presence?

Open your heart to hear God's message. Wait and rest in His presence as you absorb all that you sense and hear.

The Will: Offer words of gratitude for the truth you have experienced today concerning God's presence, His hand, and His comfort or other revelations. Write a prayer of thanksgiving in your prayer journal.

Commit to memorizing or reading daily Psalm 139:7–12 for one week.

DAY THREE: THE CHARACTER OF GOD

Two star-crossed lovers sit across a table, gazing into each other's eyes. One barely finishes talking before the other begins. It seems they just can't get enough of each other. The young pair is oblivious to the restaurant manager's anxious attempts to clean up and go home. To these two, the night has just begun as they uncover layer after layer of their true selves for each other.

If our goal is to know God, we want to know everything about Him. Like a young lover, we will stay long past closing hours, caught in the joy of exploration. And as we learn what He is like, we will experience more of His hand in our lives.

God is a fathomless being. He is a person who calls us to know Him and yet who can't be fully known. What a staggering thought: we will never run out of truth upon which to meditate.

As king of Israel, David meditated during the night when guarding his people against enemy forces. For hours alone in the darkness, he pondered the God who had called him. "I meditate on Thee in the night watches, for Thou hast been my help" (Psalm 63:6–7) .

From these times of meditation, David discovered a wealth of truth about God: He tells us God is a shelter from storms, a fountain of life, a hiding place, a fortress, a rock, a shield, a light, a righteous judge, a faithful father, and much more.

The Attributes of God

Think for a minute of the descriptions you could give God. Do you experience His love as well as His justice? His power and His meekness? His goodness and His sovereignty? His faithfulness and His mercy?

"On the glorious splendor of Thy majesty . . . I will meditate." Psalm 145 is a wellspring of wonder concerning the character of God. Orthodox Jews recite it in its entirety three times a day. It details God's omnipotence, immutability, righteousness, love, mercy, goodness, sovereignty, omnipresence, omniscience, faithfulness, and holiness. How could you be changed through meditating on these things three times every day of your life?

The Names of God

God's character is seen through His name: Jehovah—*the God who becomes*. God is all in all and yet meets each of us at our unique point of need. The Hebrew people built an altar with an inscription to Jehovah whenever they experienced His hand in a special way.

When God provided the ram and Abraham did not have to sacrifice his son, he named the place Jehovah-jireh—God my Provider. When God led the Israelites victoriously through the Red Sea, they named the altar Jehovah-nissi—The Lord our Banner.

God cannot be contained with any one title. He is El Shaddai—the all-sufficient one, and Adonai—Lord and Master. Our ability to experience a growing relationship with God will expand as we learn to meditate on Jehovah—the *God who becomes*.

The Names of God

And those who know Thy name will put their trust in Thee; for Thou, O LORD, hast not forsaken those who seek Thee (Psalm 9:10).

Jehovah-nissi *The Lord my Banner* (Exodus 17:15)
Jehovah-jireh *The Lord provides* (Genesis 22:14)
Jehovah-rapha *The Lord heals* (Exodus 15:26)
Jehovah-raah *The Lord my Shepherd* (Psalm 23)
Jehovah-shalom *The Lord our Peace* (Judges 6:24)
Jehovah-tsidkenu *The Lord our Righteousness* (Jeremiah 23:6; 33:16)
Jehovah-shammah *The Lord is present* (Ezekiel 48:35)
Jehovah-m'kaddesh *The Lord who sanctifies* (Ezekiel 36:23)
Jehovah-sabaoth *The Lord of Hosts* (Isaiah 6:3)

God Revealed

If you want to know what kind of a person God is, look at Jesus. What did He say? How did He live? How did He treat the people He encountered? What kinds of things were important to Him? Jesus was "the radiance of [God's] glory and the exact representation of His nature" (Hebrews 1:3, brackets mine).

The Gospels are a never-ending source of meditative material. Jesus said if we see Him we have seen the Father. He was God in the flesh. Just as the disciples walked and talked with Him, we can share our deepest thoughts and hear His challenging response. He calls us by name to follow Him. His words sink to the core of our soul and we are changed, as millions of followers have been since He first walked the streets of Nazareth.

Practicing Prayer: A Greater Vision of God

Heart Preparation

Take time to acknowledge God's continual presence in your life and His desire to meet with you today. Acclimate yourself. Invite the Holy Spirit to be your teacher.

The Mind: Choose one of the names of God from the chart. Look up the Scripture for that name, reading carefully. (Read the verses before and after as necessary to understand the context.) Take the time to personalize the verse.

Let your mind explore this facet of God through mental review of the following questions:

What is true about God according to this passage?

Where else have I seen this in Scripture? (Use a cross-reference if needed.)

Do I ever struggle with this concept?

Why is this attribute important?

Probe deeper with the following questions:

Why are You like this, God?

When have You demonstrated this to me?

The Heart: Quietly ask these questions:

What do you want me to know personally about this?

Have I failed to understand this or live it?

Slow your mind and seek to rest in what you know from these verses. Wait in God's presence.

Take some time to be very honest with God. Share failures, sins, discouragements, and unbelief. Confess your doubts and your desires in light of what He has revealed.

The Will: Complete any of the following thoughts that reflect your heart:

God, because this is true, I can . . .

God, because this is true, I will . . .

God, because this is true, I no longer fear . . .

God, because this is true, I am . . .

God, because this is true, I give . . .

God, because this is true, I face this day . . .

Write out what God has shown you and how it impacts your relationship with Him in your prayer journal.

Commit to reflecting on this aspect of God for a few minutes every day for one week.

DAY FOUR: THE WAYS OF GOD

Would you like to be known as "God's friend?" God spoke to Moses face-to-face, as one speaks to a friend (Exodus 33:11). How did Moses discover the kind of relationship we all long for? Knowing God was his heart's desire. Listen to his prayer: "If I have found favor in Thy sight, let me know Thy ways, *that I may know Thee . . .*" (Exodus 33:13, italics mine).

David said, "I will meditate on all Thy work and muse on Thy deeds . . . I will . . . regard Thy ways . . . on Thy wonderful works, I will meditate" (Psalms 77:12, 119:15, 145:5). As we reflect on the things God has done, we will understand and know Him more. And as we consider His ways, we are drawn to open our hearts in trust and abandonment to Him.

God's Ways in Creation

Walking along the beach, we hear the ocean's roar, its frothy surf stretching farther than we can see. We feel small and insignificant until we remember that our God has measured not just this ocean, but all the waters of the earth in the hollow of His hand. The God who walks with us also walks the worlds. God's ways in creation are beyond comprehension.

When life fills us with anxiety, we gain perspective by looking at a distant mountain range. Our God weighs the mountains in the balance and the hills in a pair of scales. When the evening news makes us feel helpless and inadequate, we rest in the truth that the nations are like a drop from a bucket and are regarded as a speck of dust on the scales of Almighty God (see Isaiah 40:15). Nothing can settle our souls like a grasp of God's greatness.

Consider His handiwork: the intricate detail of a spider web ... the aroma of a honeysuckle vine ... the fiery heat of the sun ... the terrible roar of a mountain lion ... the cry of a newborn baby.... To meditate on creation is to be filled with wonder at the God who accomplishes such incredible things.

We can only respond as David did in Psalm 8:3–4: "When I consider Thy heavens, the work of Thy fingers, the moon and the stars, which Thou hast ordained; what is man, that Thou dost take thought of him? And the son of man, that Thou dost care for him?" In realizing His vastness, we recognize our own value. Through meditation we are drawn in humble adoration and thanksgiving that He thinks of us at all.

God's Ways in the Past

A young Jewish boy comes down the stairs in great anticipation of the celebration of Passover. He has heard the story year after year, yet it never loses its excitement. He can already hear the voice of his old grandfather:

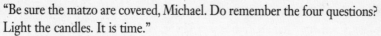

"Be sure the matzo are covered, Michael. Do remember the four questions? Light the candles. It is time."

The family solemnly gathers for the Seder. Hands are cleansed, a blessing said, one matzo divided, and the ceremony begins. The old man recites in Hebrew. Listen to the words:

> Slaves were we to Pharaoh in Egypt and the Lord our God brought us out from there with a mighty hand and an outstretched arm. If the Holy One, blessed be He, had not brought our fathers out of Egypt, then we and our children and our children's children would still be in Egypt.[4]

The story of the Exodus is repeated annually at the festival of Passover in Jewish homes throughout the world. From their inception as a nation, the Hebrew people looked for ways to recount God's hand in their lives. Psalm 136, sung by the congregation, was a litany of thanksgiving for the everlasting lovingkindness of God. Beginning with creation, detailing their own journey out of bondage, and ending with the present events, the people praised God's ways.

When David was overwhelmed with weariness and fear for his future, He called out to God: "I remember the days of old; I meditate on all Thy doing; I muse on the work of Thy hands. I stretch out my hands to Thee; My soul *longs* for Thee, as a parched land" (Psalm 143:5–6). Meditating on God's deeds in the past sustains us until we sense His work once again.

Most of us treasure special memories of God providing for us in a unique way. Perhaps it was in the midst of a long struggle or during times of discouragement and doubt. For me there are many: the time my oldest sister came home, broken and disillusioned from a life of drugs to commit her life to Christ . . . the day when as a young missionary in an Alaskan village I saw my first Eskimo friend give her heart to God . . . the evening the phone rang with an offer of a baby to adopt after years of painful infertility . . . so many memories, I visit them often. They have become altars in my heart from which I worship God and remember His ways.

We gain perspective as we look at the scope of our life, recognizing all that God has done—perhaps when we weren't even aware. And like David, we will ask for the privilege of declaring God's wondrous deeds even when we are old and gray (Psalm 71:17–18).

Practicing Prayer: This I Recall

Heart Preparation

Acknowledge that God is with you and desires to speak today. Acclimate yourself. Ask the Holy Spirit to lead into all truth.

The Mind: Read Psalm 136 through slowly, aloud.

Spend some time looking back through your life. Remember when God touched you, revealed himself, or provided in a unique way. Take the time to think of several things. In your prayer journal, write your own psalm of thanksgiving. Begin with general things, such as His goodness, His power, His acts in creation. Then move to your own life. Write down what He has done. After each declaration, write: *For His lovingkindness is everlasting.*

The Heart: Read your psalm aloud. Let your mind ponder the ways of God reflected in it. Receive the love He continues to pour out today. Say aloud: *Your lovingkindness is everlasting,* a few times. Let this thought take root.

The Will: Look forward to the day ahead. Respond to what you have seen and experienced. Complete the sentence: Lord, I face this day with a fresh awareness that . . .

DAY FIVE: THE WORD OF GOD

A red chest with mother-of-pearl etchings stands in the closet of my bedroom. It is the keeper of my most precious possessions, including a small stack of love letters from my husband. His first letter is the most precious to me. An awkward nineteen-year-old, newly in love, begins his romantic endeavor with these words: *Well, I've never written a love letter before, but I guess this is as good a time as any to try.* How I treasured those fifteen lines he eked out. I kept them by my bed and read them every night for weeks.

The Nature of God's Word

God's Word is a love letter written for the heart of His beloved. It is a treasure—a gift like no other. He hopes we will hold it close, finding joy in every word day after day after day. David did, and cried out: "O how I love Thy law! It is my meditation all the day" (Psalm 119:97).

Is it hard for you to relate to this kind of passion? Perhaps you feel you have studied, memorized, or even taught God's Word, and yet it doesn't seem to have the impact you desire. Maybe you have little longing for it at all and your greatest attempts at discipline concerning Scripture have been weak and inconsistent.

The difficulty may be in the way you approach God's Word. In Meditative Prayer the Bible is not a rule book, a history lesson, or a treatise to be dissected and analyzed. We come to its Author with our hearts open and our desire for *Him*. Over and over in the Psalms, David poured out his yearning for God's Word, that he might know and serve Him with all his heart.

How blessed are those who observe His testimonies, who seek Him with all their heart (Psalm 119:2).

With all my heart I have sought Thee (Psalm 119:10).

Thy word I have treasured in my heart (Psalm 119:11).

My soul is crushed with longing after Thine ordinances at all times (Psalm 119:20).

May my heart be blameless in Thy statutes (Psalm 119:80).

We can hide God's Word in our hearts through Meditative Prayer. Seeking God's face, we want to understand the person who wrote these powerful words. Our hearts are the soil in which the Word is planted. Every part of our being joins together to nourish the seeds of truth until they sprout and bring life to our soul.

The Power of God's Word

There is no better source for Meditative Prayer than the Word of God. The earliest believers loved God's Word and felt it "revealed the secret movements of the heart in its struggle against the forces of darkness."[5]

Meditation for them was almost entirely *meditatio scripturarum*—a focus on the pure Word of God.

A Russian peasant from the seventeenth century introduced a meaningful form of meditation from God's Word called the *Jesus Prayer*. Through months of prayerful meditation on the publican's prayer: "God, be merciful to me, the sinner!" (Luke 18:13), the peasant's life was transformed.[6]

This ancient prayer is still practiced among Eastern Orthodox believers. Reflecting on one word at a time, they seek to comprehend God's great mercy and their vast need.

Other phrases from Scripture can also be used to pray in this way. The key is to concentrate on a couple of phrases, one word at a time. Once you have focused on it in prayer, you can practice throughout the day—driving to work, making lunch, doing dishes, or getting dressed.

Scripture is replete with phrases and promises upon which we can meditate. Dick Eastman notes that there are over 30,000 promises and thousands of brief phrases that inspire enormous power.[7] If we want to know the heart of God, we need only meditate on His letter of love to us.

Reading, studying or memorizing God's Word will only take us so far in our quest for spiritual growth. Letting God saturate our inner selves with His truth requires a heart that wants more than guidelines for living. We invite the giver of Scripture to come in, to sup with us and we with Him. And in the fellowship we share, we are loved, embraced, and changed by our Lord himself.

Practicing Prayer: A Mystery

Heart Preparation

Acknowledge that God is present and wants to be your teacher. Invite His work in every part of your life. Acclimate yourself. Ask the Holy Spirit to reveal truth today.

The Mind: Read Colossians 1:25–27. Look up these cross-references: Romans 8:10; 1 Timothy 1:6–7.

Focus on the word *mystery*.

>What do you think of when you hear the word mystery?
>
>What does it mean? (Look it up in a dictionary.)
>
>Read verse 27 very slowly, aloud.
>
>What does this verse say the mystery is?
>
>Why is this a mystery?

Ponder these thoughts:

>Who lives within me?
>
>How is this possible?
>
>What does this mean?
>
>Why should this give me hope?

The Heart: Say quietly several times: "Christ in me, the hope of glory." Ask God to plant this truth deep within.

Slow your mind to reflect on what you hear Him saying.

Rest here, waiting, listening and experiencing His presence.

The Will: Ask:

Lord, how does my life reflect this truth?

How does my life deny it?

What are you calling me to believe?

What are you asking me to do?

Write a letter of response in your prayer journal.

Moving Forward

In our last chapter we established some discipline and commitment for our inner prayer journey. This chapter opened our box of tools to teach us how to meditate in prayer. You may want to spend more time developing your own meditations before going on. Keep Meditative Prayer a regular part of your prayer journey. We have studied it first because it is foundational.

In the next chapter, we will learn how God enlivens our imagination to comprehend His Word completely. Through Scripture Praying, we experience the pages of God's Word as if we were there the moment it was God-breathed. God's written Word will become our living Word as we walk within its sphere, embracing fully the life He offers.

Notes

1. Andrew Murray, *The Believer's Daily Renewal* (Minneapolis: Bethany House Publishers, 1981), p. 54.
2. Murray, p. 57.
3. Eddie Ensley, *Prayer That Heals Our Emotions* (San Francisco: Harper and Row, 1988), p. 12.
4. Taken from the Haggadah, traditional liturgy for Passover.
5. Thomas Merton, *Contemplative Prayer* (New York: Herder and Herder, 1969), p. 22.
6. Anonymous, *The Way of Pilgrim* and *The Pilgrim Continues His Way* (New York: Doubleday/Image, 1979).
7. Dick Eastman, *The Hour That Changes the World* (Grand Rapids: Baker Books, 1978), p. 120.

CHAPTER THREE

SCRIPTURE PRAYING

The Bible—its light is like the body of heaven in its clearness;
Its vastness like the bosom of the sea;
Its variety like scenes
of nature.

John Henry Newman

The Bible and Us

A single, thirty-four-year-old businesswoman reads stories of women in the Old Testament who were the property of their husbands and thinks Scripture may be *irrelevant* to her lifestyle. A high school senior is tired of searching God's Word for answers regarding which college to attend and thinks the Bible must be *impractical* for daily decision-making. A middle-aged recovering alcoholic approaches the Bible with timidity, usually hearing angry voices of condemnation.

Irrelevant, impractical, and judgmental. What are your feelings concerning God's Word? James 1:21 says: "In humility receive the word." To *receive*, means to approach with a welcoming embrace. Would you like to come to Scripture with arms wide open, welcoming it like a trusted friend?

Passion for God's Word permeates Psalm 119: "How sweet are Thy words to my taste! *Yes, sweeter* than honey to my mouth!" (v. 103). "My eyes anticipate the night watches, that I may meditate on Thy word" (v. 148). "Therefore I love Thy commandments above gold, yes, above fine gold"

(v. 127). "I opened my mouth wide and panted, for I longed for Thy commandments" (v. 131).

Jack Hayford, a well-known pastor, once said that when he went on vacation, he couldn't wait for a quiet time and place to read the Scripture. This man makes his living studying the Bible and yet never tires of it. Why is it so tantalizing to him? How do seeds of desire blossom into a longing like his?

The Story of the Bible

God pursuing man—that is the theme of His written Word. Think of it:

Crazy Noah building an ark . . .

Stunned Moses at the burning bush . . .

Fearful Jeremiah questioning God's call . . .

Teenage Mary, a virgin yet pregnant . . .

Boisterous Peter leaving his nets . . .

Ambitious Paul struck blind. . . .

The story is spun in historical accounts from the garden of Eden to Revelation's mighty throne room. It is painted in pictures passed on through prophets and priests, and in parables spoken by Jesus the Teacher.

Scripture Praying is a rendezvous with God among the pages of this incredible book. He calls us by name to take part in the unfolding drama. The God of Abraham and Moses thunders and His words ignite a flame of faith within us. Walking the streets of Jerusalem with Jesus, we draw closer to His side.

The Story of the Bible and Prayer

Every year, Laguna Beach, California, hosts a celebration of art called *The Pageant of the Masters*, in which famous paintings by artists such as Van

Gogh and Da Vinci are brought to life. The set is constructed with attention to the finest detail. Actors are groomed and dressed with careful authenticity. When the curtain opens, the audience is transported to another time and place as great moments of art history are recreated.

Scripture Praying is a lot like that. We step into the Bible's pictures, parables, and encounters with God, like participants in a story where the ink on the pages hasn't had time to dry. The Author is there to meet us. This experience opens our eyes to horizons we've never scanned. A new world arises, as A. W. Tozer says, "out of the religious mists, when we approach our Bible with the idea that it is not only a book that was once spoken, but a book that is now speaking."[1]

DAY ONE: SOURCES

The Gift of Imagination

Imagination is a gift from God—a reminder that we are made in His image. God moves in mystery and wonder: He speaks into the void and light breaks through. He creates a flawless world and risks its destruction. He enters humanity as a babe in a barn, heralded by an angel choir. We will never fully comprehend His ways, but through our imagination we develop a sense of wonder for all He is and does.

With abandon, let your mind travel through God's Word until it is your personal journey. Smell the salty air by the Sea of Galilee or hear the thundering roar of the Egyptian army at your back as you flee captivity. Touch the scars on the Savior's side or taste His tears in the Garden of Gethsemane. Lay your head on His breast and hear His heartbeat. This is Scripture Praying.

~ ~

Is Visualization a New Age Practice?

There has been much misinformation regarding the use of imagination or visualization in our Christian life. Consider these important distinctions:

- *In Scripture Praying, God's Word is reality; visualization is simply a tool to help us fully embrace it, while New Age visualization seeks to create its own reality through the force of one's mind.*
- *In Scripture Praying, we depend on the Holy Spirit to guide our imagination safely within the confines of Scripture, while New Age visualization calls its participants to become like God, depending on themselves to chart their own future.*

We should not let their abuse rob us of a God-given resource.

Categories for Scripture Praying

We learned in the last chapter how to use God's Word in Meditative Prayer. Scripture Praying differs in that we experience God's presence through visualization based on His Word. There are at least three categories from which we can draw: Bible characters, pictures, and parables.

Bible Characters and Events

Nothing makes Scripture come to life like getting to know its key players. We don't stand back observing or analyzing, but jump into the fray, exploring and personalizing their experiences. What was *Noah* really like? Did he chafe under the ridicule of a pagan world? How do I respond when God calls me to obedience that looks like insanity?

What happened to *Moses* when God spoke from the burning bush? Was it unbearably hot? Did his heart pound and his palms become sweaty in the isolation of that mountain? When God shakes my ordered world, do I turn from the heat or choose to pursue His friendship?

Blind *Bartimaeus*. What must it have been like to have known only darkness all his life, and with one touch from the Master see every hue and shape in our multicolored world? What kind of darkness did I know before Christ? How has His healing touch transformed me?

Each of these encounters are filled with life-changing lessons we learn through Scripture Praying. We become so engulfed in the experience that we cannot help but respond to the God who is exposed through it.

Alexander Whyte, a Scottish preacher whose reputation for fiery oration was well known in the late 1800s, challenged his hearers with their approach to Scripture. In one sermon he pleads:

> Never hear a chapter of the Gospel read without seeing, as if you had been there, all that is read about. Be, for a time, in Bethlehem, in Nazareth, in Galilee, in Jerusalem, and in the Garden, on Golgotha and Olivet. Never see His name, even written in pen or pencil, and never hear His name in a sermon or in a psalm or a prayer, without seeing His face at the same time and falling down before Him.[2]

Bible Pictures

God longs for us to know Him in a tangible way. To this end, He has painted hundreds of self-portraits for us to peruse. He is a fountain of living water, a shelter from the storm, a vinedresser, a shepherd, the Lion of Judah, and a potter. He is a sacrificial lamb, a mighty warrior, a bruised reed, the Lily of the Valley, a sure foundation, and a root out of dry ground. He is the Bright and Morning Star, faithful lover, the Great Physician, the Bread of Life, and the Light of the World. This endless list makes one thing clear: God is so vast, so broad, so incredibly complex that we will spend an entire lifetime getting to know Him and yet face eternity with anticipation.

In Scripture Praying, we take one of these images and explore it. We visualize ourselves within the picture, experiencing it until its truth becomes a part of us. One entry in my prayer journal reflects a time of Scripture Praying that has had a powerful impact on my life. I read Jeremiah 18:4: "[The potter] remade it into another vessel, as it pleased the potter to make" (brackets mine). I looked up related verses: Isaiah 45:9; 64:8; Matthew 20:15; Romans 9:21.

I saw myself as clay on the potter's wheel, but couldn't stay there. I climbed off over and over again because the process of being broken and remade was simply too hard. The words of the old hymn "Have Thine Own Way" played a haunting melody in my mind.

I knew I must be broken, forcibly pulled to the center of the wheel, and I grieved at my resistance. Finally I saw myself climbing back on and felt God's hands of love—firm and purposeful. I wrote: *Lord, I don't want to remove myself for one minute. I don't want to question you by my words or actions. I want to be in your hands to be fashioned as you will. You are the Potter, I am the clay.*

Throughout that day and many following I placed the pieces of my life— my dreams, ambitions, family, ministry, time, talent, and hopes on the potter's wheel. This made a lasting impression. Now, when I struggle with God's plan, I remember that the master Potter is making me into the image of His Son and I find peace.

Bible Parables

A parable is a story that illustrates truth. Our task is to take hold of the story until the truth it represents takes hold of us. Jesus was the master teacher of parables, although some parables were imparted through the prophets.

Isaiah tells of a vineyard that has been tenderly planted and cared for by its owner. He fenced it in, planted the best seeds in rich soil, and built a winepress nearby so the grapes would be fresh from harvest. But this vineyard produced worthless grapes, so the vinedresser took away his protective fence, letting his precious vineyard be laid waste (Isaiah 5:1–7).

In Scripture Praying, we might see our lives as the vineyard and Jesus as the vinedresser. We can feel His tender hand carefully planting the seeds of His Word in our hearts. We sense the security of His constant care and growth under His guidance. We may be drawn to examine the fruit in our own lives—is it good fruit? Has God removed His protection because of our indifference or rebellion?

The book of Hosea is in many ways a parable of God's faithfulness. It tells of Hosea's unconditional love and commitment to his wife even in the face of her infidelity and rejection. Through Scripture Prayer, this story reveals God as our faithful Lover. Looking back on our life, we recall the times we have rejected Him, wandering away to pursue our own pleasure. Then we hear His voice saying, "I will heal [your] apostasy, I will love [you] freely, for My anger has turned away from [you]" (Hosea 14:4, brackets mine).

The parables of Jesus are a wonderful source for Scripture Praying. Each one offers a unique perspective on our relationship to God. We grow in security as we become the Wandering Lamb or the Lost Coin. The House on the Rock reminds us to consider our life's priorities, while the Mustard Seed encourages us to exercise even the tiniest bit of faith. The Sower, the Persistent Widow, the Ten Virgins, the Unjust Judge, and many others provide a way for us to know the mind of Christ more fully.

Parables of Jesus for Scripture Praying

The Friend at Midnight—Luke 11:5–13
The Pearl of Great Price—Matthew 13:45–46
The Great Supper—Luke 14:16–24
The Hidden Treasure—Matthew 13:44
The Laborers in the Vineyard—Matthew 20:1–16
The Pharisee and Publican—Luke 18:9–15
The Piece of Money—Luke 15:8–10
The Prodigal Son—Luke 15:11–32
The Rich Fool—Luke 12:16–31
The Seed Growing in Secret—Mark 4:21–29
The Sheep and Goats—Matthew 25:31–46
The Tares—Matthew 13:24–43
The Ten Talents—Matthew 25:14–30
The Two Debtors—Luke 7:40–47
The Two Sons—Matthew 21:28–32
The Unjust Steward—Luke 16:1–13
The Unmerciful Servant—Matthew 18:21–35
The Unprofitable Servants—Luke 17:7–10
The Wedding Feast—Luke 14:7–15
The Wise Steward—Luke 12:35–48
The House on the Rock—Matthew 7:24–29
The Lost Sheep—Matthew 18:11–14
The New Cloth—Mark 2:21–22
The New Wine—Mark 2:22
The Sower—Luke 8:4–15

Scripture Praying can be as simple as a prayer or as complex as in-depth Bible study. The key is to come to God's Word as a participant, ready to experience firsthand all that takes place within its pages. Through your imagination, immerse yourself in biblical truth until your heart is moved. For now, we will take an event from Scripture, personalize and internalize it, and deepen our commitment to knowing Christ through Scripture Prayer.

Practicing Prayer: A Child in His Arms

Heart Preparation

Read Mark 10:13–16 and Matthew 18:2–4 at least twice.

Write out Jesus' words concerning children in your prayer journal.

Close your eyes for a few minutes and become acclimated to the presence of God. Acknowledge your own need as a child—your complete dependency on Him. Share with Him any fears and concerns. You might want to pray the following or write your own prayer:

> *Thank you Father God for your perfect, unending love. I want to be your child but I'm not even sure I know how to come to You. Help me to understand my own need and increase my trust so I can learn to rest in Your arms.*

Read the passage from Mark one more time. Find a comfortable place to sit and breathe in God's love. Breathe out distractions or anxieties. (Practice this until you are relaxed and ready to visualize the story.) Read the following description once or twice until the scene is clear in your mind. Then close your eyes and visualize yourself as a part of the experience.

Feel the bright sun shining. . . . Smell the fresh clean scent of nature. . . . Sense the spontaneity of children. . . . Hear their laughter. . . . See parents proudly holding out their young ones. . . . Look at the face of Jesus, laughing, holding, blessing the children. Now, see yourself as a child going toward Him. See Him smiling, holding out His arms, beckoning you to come. He looks into your eyes. How do you respond? Do you run toward Him? Walk timidly? Wait for Him to take your hand? See yourself climbing into His lap. He cradles you in His arms, drawing you close to His heart. Can you imagine Him holding your face with one hand, the other hand resting on your head? He wants to bless you like He has the other children. Allow all other sounds to fade away as you hear Him speak directly to you. What might He say? Listen carefully. . . .

Spend some time experiencing His love. If you can, sing softly: *Jesus loves me, this I know.* . . .

DAY TWO: FRAME

My oldest son loves to surf. One day I went along, excited about taking pictures with our new camera. Standing near the water as he paddled out, I waited eagerly for him to catch his first wave. After a few false starts, he got up, maneuvering the board back and forth across the wave. Enchanted by the ocean's roar and my son's dexterity, I shot an entire roll of film. But when we had it developed, every picture was the same—a blue mass dotted with black specks.

What had I done wrong? I had failed to *frame* my subject. Every good photographer knows that *framing* is the first step. You look at the big picture, establish a target point of interest, choose the best angle, and zoom in on the subject. A failure to *frame* your shot leaves you with lots of distractions and no clear picture.

A friend once told me she loved nothing better than to read large portions of Scripture in one sitting. Just that morning she had read fifteen chapters from the book of Exodus. I asked her what spoke to her the most. Her answer was interesting but had little to do with God's work in her own life. While every exposure to Scripture is valuable, when we *frame* a passage we open ourselves to God's Word on a more personal level.

Look at the Big Picture

In Scripture Praying, we *frame* the passage much as a photographer frames his subject. Looking first at the big picture, we examine God's Word by asking key questions:

Who is involved in this story or described through these words?

Where did it take place?

What is going on or what is the context for these words? What is the setting?

When did this take place?

How does God work in this passage?

Why was this passage written?

At times it is helpful to read several verses before and after the passage, or other related passages. (Refer to your Bible's cross-reference.) Some other helpful tools are a concordance, Bible dictionary, and commentary. But often all the information you need is within the passage itself.

Choose Your Angle

Once you have the big picture, you are ready to choose an angle. In Scripture Praying, we decide what specific point of view we would like to pursue. For example, the story of the Prodigal Son can center on the father, the son, or even the angry brother. There are lessons to learn from the lives of each one. This does not minimize the other people or events in the passage. It simply means, for this time, we want to completely grasp the truth from one angle or perspective.

Using a Scripture Meditation Journal

The purpose of this journal is a little different than that of your prayer journal. In this one, you record truths, lessons, and other juicy morsels that God shows you from His Word. Use it for Scripture Praying, Meditative Prayer, and later for Listening Prayer.

Zoom in on Your Subject

A photographer stands in the rain, juggling his umbrella and tripod, as he tries to capture the mountain storm for the daily newspaper. He frames his first shot—several young pine trees, bent and almost breaking against the wind. A series of rocks jut out of the ground below, oblivious to the shaking all around them. Clutching the lens, he adjusts the focus and movement catches his eye.

He zooms in closer. The trees disappear as he examines a single rock, shaped like a fat letter C. In the center, unaware of any danger, a tiny squirrel sorts his store of nuts. He picks one up and nibbles on it. CLICK. *The Daily News*, page three, displays the picture with the caption: "The Eye of the Storm."

We do a similar thing by zooming in on our subject in Scripture Praying. This is important to determine which aspect addresses our personal need. As we zoom in closer, we ask more specific questions based on the uniqueness of this person's experience.

Our goal is to get as close to the subject as we can, yet maintaining a clear picture. The news photographer moved past the heavy hitting rain, the wind beaten trees, and the boulders surrounding them. By zooming in on the squirrel, he gave depth and meaning to otherwise typical storm footage. In *framing* we let other things go as we hone in on the heart of the perspective we have chosen.

Practicing Prayer: Getting the Big Picture

For the next several devotionals we will look at the same passage. Today we will *frame it*, then in the coming lessons, we will learn to *focus it*, *capture it*, and *develop it*.

Heart Preparation

Spend a few minutes acclimating yourself. Turn this time over to the Lord, claiming in faith the promise that He will reveal truth through His Word to you.

Read the Scripture Passage (Luke 17:11–19) at least two times.

Frame: Answer the following questions to establish the big picture:

Who is involved in this story and what does the passage tell you about them? (See 2 Kings 17:24–39; Luke 9:51–53; John 4:9 for more information concerning Samaritans and their relationship to the Jews.)

Where does the story take place? You might use a Bible map to find its location and a Bible dictionary to tell you more about the specific place.

For further information, read the passages before and after to determine where Jesus had been and where He was going next.

What is going on in the story?

(See Leviticus 13:43–59 for explanation of the leper's status and relationship to priests.)

When did this take place? (Time of day, in relationship to Jesus' time on earth, etc.)

How does God work in this passage? Be sure to look at all the people involved—how are they impacted, changed?

Review your notes as you begin to choose your angle. Prayerfully decide whose perspective you would like to understand. Is it that of the nine who weren't thankful? The one who was? Jesus? The disciples who watched? The priests who had to declare them healed? Others? Once you have decided, consider the following questions:

What was unique to this person's experience?

What might he have been like before this happened?

What else do we know about his history, if anything?

Is the location significant?

How does the setting for this event play an important role?

As you think through these questions, write down any other things that help clarify the frame you have chosen.

Ask God to make this story real to you in the coming days.

DAY THREE: FOCUS

We have all known the frustration of fuzzy photos. They're not only lousy to look at—they're worthless. A photo lab can make corrections for various errors by cropping, enlarging, or enhancing, but they can do nothing about a picture that is out of focus. Good photographers take time to ensure the subject matter is clear before the picture is taken.

Taking the Time

Do you ever study the Bible and end up with a hazy picture of what God is saying? Do you struggle to remember today what you learned yesterday?

This is why we need to *focus* through Scripture Prayer. A photographer adjusts his lens until the subject stands out with precision and clarity. In the same way, we *focus* in on a passage until it grabs our attention and every detail is clear. We do not move on until this happens.

Letting the Light In

Begin the *focus* process with prayer. Ephesians 1:18 says: "I pray that the eyes of your heart may be enlightened. . . ." As the photographer enhances the focus by letting in more light, you will see more clearly by inviting God's light to shine so that His words are permanently imprinted on your heart like pictures on a roll of film.

Experience the Word

Next, fine tune your understanding of the passage by asking things like:
What is really going on from this angle?
How are people feeling?
What are they seeing? Hearing? Touching?
What would I be feeling, seeing, hearing or touching if I were there?
Place yourself within the experience and you will gain incredible insight. Read of the man by the pool of Bethesda, and see your own brokenness as Jesus asks, "Do you want to be made whole?" Don't scoff at the rich young ruler who wouldn't give all to follow Jesus, but face your own capacity to turn from the face of a loving Savior. Read of young David who refused someone else's armor, winning the battle with a few stones. Examine whose abilities, methods, or talents you have tried to use in your personal battles.

Photography at its best captures more than surface images. It delves into the hidden words, secret fears, or painful experiences of its subjects.

What did Samuel think about God calling his name in the dark?

Was he afraid? In awe?

Did he believe he was imagining things?

Have I ever thought I heard God's voice?

Could I tell someone, or was I afraid they'd laugh?

How many times does God have to call for me to respond, "Here I am"?

What might Peter have felt when he wept bitterly over betraying Christ? Had he lost all hope? Given up on himself? Was he consumed with self-hatred?

How do I respond when facing spiritual failure? Do I run from God in shame? Am I callous, or so beaten down I can't believe He could love me?

These are the kinds of questions we pursue in our efforts to find personal *focus* from God's Word.

Practicing Prayer: God Speaks to You

Heart Preparation

Spend some time in prayer before God, asking Him to shine His light into your heart and to open your spiritual eyes to comprehend truth. Commit the process to Him. Read the passage (Luke 17:11–19) again. Meditatively review your notes from the *Frame* section.

Focus:

Focusing specifically on the angle you have chosen, consider these questions:

What is the atmosphere like? The sounds? Smells? Sights?

Take time to really comprehend what it would have been like to have been there at that moment.

How did the person react or respond to the given situation? Does the passage tell you? If not, what might have been his or her response?

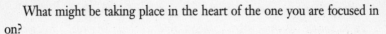

What might be taking place in the heart of the one you are focused in on?

How might this person be feeling about the situation as it develops?

What is he or she seeing that is unique to his or her perspective?

What may have been his or her inner secrets or fears?

If you were that person, what would you have been feeling?

How would this experience have impacted your life?

Write any further ideas that enable you to focus in on the subject you have framed. He or she should now stand out with clarity as you find yourself identifying some part of your own life with the experience described here.

DAY FOUR: CAPTURE

Every year, on our anniversary, we wipe the dust off our wedding pictures and relive those precious memories. One picture in particular always floods me with fresh emotion. Moments before the wedding, I stood gazing out a second-story window as people arrived. Anticipating this milestone in my life, I was filled with wonder. The photographer caught this as she took a picture unbeknownst to me. Then she juxtaposed that image of my face on a picture taken from the balcony of the church during the wedding. It was as if I were watching my own wedding in wonder. This picture always reminds me of the way I felt that day.

Seize the Moment

The most important element for any photographer is knowing when to take the picture. He *frame*s and *focus*es his subject until intuitively he senses the time is right. This is the image he wants to preserve—an *Aha!* moment. Absolutely still, he glances through the lens one more time. The angle is right, the picture clear, distractions removed, and the light sufficient. He takes the picture—a moment in time preserved for posterity.

In Scripture Praying, there comes a time when we are ready to *capture* the essence of the passage we have *framed* and *focused*. Perhaps we have had some sense of having been there, or of a significant, related moment in our own life. Like the photographer's *aha!* God's touch transforms the ordinary and we must savor it.

Preserve the Experience

This time should never be rushed. There will be a stillness, a point at which you want to imprint the image deep within. Lay aside all other cares or needs and hear what God says.

Allow yourself to fully embrace His message with your mind and your emotions. Laugh, cry, hold your hands up, fall on your knees or raise your face to the light of His presence. Look to Him, hear Him. "This can be more than an exercise of the imagination; it can be a genuine confrontation."[3]

Through prayerful meditation, write His words on your heart. Sometimes in silence, sometimes in words of praise and thanksgiving, sometimes in conviction and repentance, experience the presence of God, taking as much time as necessary to internalize the image. You have *captured* the heartbeat of God.

Practicing Prayer: The "Aha" Moment

Heart Preparation

This part of the devotional should be done in one sitting. You will probably need about thirty minutes. Read the passage (Luke 17:11–19) again. Review your notes from the *Frame* and *Focus* sections, prayerfully seeking

God's plan. You may want to read through the following words a couple of times. Offer yourself to God, asking His Holy Spirit to fill your heart and mind with His truth and light. Breathe deeply, allowing the distractions of life to slowly fade away. Still and quiet your soul before God.

Capture: Relive the passage from Scripture in your mind. Experience with your emotions the full extent of what is happening within the frame you have chosen. Prayerfully meditate, allowing yourself to see as others saw, to hear as others heard, and to be moved as they were through this encounter.

Remember that you are in the presence of God. Is there one significant moment or thought from the passage? In the stillness and quietness of this time, allow yourself to examine it carefully.

Listen for God's voice. He will write His message on your heart with a permanent imprint. Capture this moment by internalizing the truth in meditation.

As you spend this time in His presence, you will feel drawn to respond in some way. If you sense nothing specific, ask God to reveal to you what He sees within your heart.

Is there conviction of sin you long to confess?

Are you drawn to pour out praise and thanksgiving?

Do you feel peace just resting in silence before God?

Through prayer and meditation, allow these things to surface.

Spend some time actively engaging in dialogue with God concerning all He has shown you. Write a love letter of response in your journal.

DAY FIVE: DEVELOP

We preserve God's message to us by *developing* it. Just as a roll of film left lying in a drawer fades with time, lessons learned through Scripture

Praying lose their value when not *developed* for further use. We need to take steps to make it tangible, passing it on to others. There are several ways to do this.

Quick Reference Guide for Scripture Praying

FRAME IT: *Look at the Big Picture*
               Choose Your Angle
               Zoom in on Your Subject
FOCUS IT: *Take the Time to Fine Tune*
               Let the Light in Through Prayer
               Experience the Word
CAPTURE IT: *Seize the Moment*
               Preserve the Experience
DEVELOP IT: *Look for Related Truth*
               Write Reflections in Journal
               Choose a Key Verse
               Relive the Experience
               Pass It On

Look for Related Truth

First, look for related Scriptures, depending on the angle you have chosen. If you have been impressed with the courage of someone who came to Jesus, find verses on courage to read for follow-up. If you have experienced God as a Shepherd, look for verses on guidance and protection. This will secure the message, and keep you from forming conclusions that are not reflected elsewhere in Scripture.

Write Personal Reflections in Journal

Another way to develop the truth is to ask meditative questions, writing your responses in a journal. Some possibilities are:

What have I really learned from this experience?

How will my life be impacted by these truths?

What will I do as a result of this meditation?

How has my understanding of God changed through this?

Choose a Key Verse

Choose a key verse from or related to the message of the Scripture passage. Write it on a card that you can keep with you for the next several days. Read it aloud several times, personalizing it by placing your name where appropriate. For example:

Do not fear (JOHN), for I am with you; do not anxiously look about you, for I am your God. I will strengthen (JOHN), surely I will help (JOHN). Surely I will uphold (JOHN) with My righteous right hand (Isaiah 41:10).

Memorize the verse if possible. This puts the truth in front of you until it becomes permanently written on your heart.

Relive the Scripture Prayer Experience

Finally, commit to meditating on the message God has given at least three more times in the coming weeks. As you come to your quiet time, read the passage if you need to, then move to the *Capture* section. Ask God to reestablish it within your heart. This will bring about real change.

Pass It On

Even amateur photographers find great joy in sharing their treasured moments on film with others. When we look at God's message with someone else, we are able to experience it again, just as if we are reliving a special event. This benefits us the most, but also has the power to greatly influence other lives. As Jesus said, "Freely you have received, freely give" (Matthew 10:8)

Practicing Prayer: Making It Last

Heart Preparation

Spend a few minutes in prayer, seeking God's power to do what He calls you to do. Read through your notes from the previous three sections. Spend a few minutes reexperiencing the *Capture* section.

Develop:

Ask these or other meditative questions, writing your responses in a journal.

What have I really learned from this experience?

How will my life be impacted by these truths?

What will I do as a result of this time of Scripture Praying?

How has my understanding of God or myself changed through this?

Depending on the angle you have used, find related Scriptures to read and study. Select a key word and use your concordance. For example, you might look at the words *gratitude, rejection, hope, healing,* or others unique to what God has taught you.

List the related Scriptures in your journal.

Choose a key verse from the passage or the related verses.

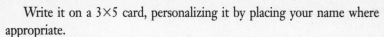

Write it on a 3×5 card, personalizing it by placing your name where appropriate.

Be committed to memorizing the verse by reading it aloud two or three times a day.

Make a commitment to *revisit* the passage at least twice in the coming week. As you come to your quiet time, go right to the *Capture* section. Ask God to reestablish it within your heart.

Experience it again, allowing the truth to sink deeper.

Share with a trusted friend or small group (Support, Bible Study, Sunday school) what God has taught you through this passage.

Moving Forward

We have now learned two different tools for our inner prayer journey. Scripture Prayer and Meditative Prayer support each other. It may be helpful for you to pursue your own times of Scripture Praying before you try to move to the next chapter. Learn of God's character through pictures,* His love through the parables and His ways through Bible events. This immersion in the Word of God establishes your inner prayer journey on a firm foundation rather than empty emotionalism.

Our next tool opens us to an exciting venture, which may be new for some. God speaks every day to each of His children. He longs for us to stop and listen to what He has to say. Jesus said His sheep hear Him and know His voice. In Listening Prayer, we learn how to be still enough to hear Him and be sure it is His voice speaking. As we learn to listen to our Gentle Shepherd through the valleys, mountains, and meadows of our lives, we will affirm with confidence that we are His lambs.

---

*Many Bible pictures and parables do not require the extensive *Frame* or *Focus* sections. Apply instead the components of Meditative Prayer (mind, heart, and will), and then move to the *Capture* and *Develop* sections.

Notes

1. A. W. Tozer, *The Pursuit of God* (Camp Hill, Penn.: Christian Publications Inc., 1948), p. 82.
2. Alexander Whyte, *Lord, Teach Us to Pray* (New York: George H. Doran Company), p. 100.
3. Richard Foster, *Celebration of Discipline* (San Francisco: Harper and Row: 1978), p. 26.

Chapter Four
Listening Prayer

Blessed is the man who listens to me,
Watching daily at my gates,
Waiting at my doorposts
(Proverbs 8:34).
Lord! deliver me from the uncircumcised ear.

Andrew Murray

A hand crept up in the back row—a quiet young woman who had considered my teaching on prayer for two days. She hesitated. "How do you know when God is speaking to you? I don't think I've ever heard Him."

A woman nearby quipped, "Yeah. I always get a little nervous when people say God told them something. I mean, if they're hearing from God, I figure three's a crowd and I better get out of there."

The group of women laughed, but expectancy filled the air as they awaited my response. It was as if I had uttered a mystery and might now reveal it's secret. In light of the discussion that followed, I realized how many people don't experience the joy of hearing God on a regular basis. While Jesus promised that we would hear *and* know His voice, some feel this is too mystical or must apply to the "super-spiritual."

Does God speak to you? Do His words and impressions shape your life, or does this experience sound mysterious or unsettling? Wherever your journey has led thus far, God has new vistas for you to explore through Listening Prayer.

God's Voice in Scripture

While the voice of God throughout the Bible varies in intensity, tone, and message, clearly God communicates in a way his creatures can hear and understand. The evening after they sinned in the Garden of Eden, Adam and Eve heard the voice of God and ran to hide. God told Noah to build an ark, and Abram to leave home for an unknown destination. He called the young Samuel in the middle of the night and whispered to Elijah after a mighty earthquake. Moses heard God from the burning bush, Isaiah heard him in the temple after a glorious time of worship, and prophet after prophet imparted to a rebellious people the words God spoke to them in private.

How did they hear God? Did He speak out loud? What did it sound like? How were they sure it was God? Experiences differ throughout Scripture. How God speaks will become clearer as we go along. The key issue is that God spoke and people responded. If He spoke to them, surely He speaks to us.

God's Heart for Us to Hear

What is God's heart concerning Listening Prayer? He wants us to hear Him more than any works we might do in His Name (Psalm 40:6). He blesses us when we hear what He has to say (Matthew 13:16–17). God makes our ears to hear (Proverbs 20:12) and calls us to listen, rather than ramble with wordiness in His presence (Ecclesiastes 5:1–2). Jesus said our ability to follow Him is dependent on our willingness to hear His voice. He makes no exception to the rule: "My sheep hear My voice, and I know them, and they follow Me" (John 10:27).

Perhaps the greatest indication of God's longing for us to hear Him is found in Jesus' words to his beloved John on the Isle of Patmos. Hear His heart:

> Stop and listen, my child. What do you hear? I am standing right here at the entrance to your soul, longing to come in. But I must wait—knocking . . . knocking . . . knocking . . .
>
> Can you hear my gentle call? I want to hear your joys and sorrows, victories and defeats. . . . But I also long to unveil my heart—my hurts, joys, plans and purposes for this day in your life. Will you invite me in? (Paraphrase of Revelation 3:20.)

This is God's desire—a relationship of give and take, of sharing and hearing, of listening and responding. He will speak to anyone who will take the time to listen. Do you want to hear Him?

DAY ONE: HOW GOD SPEAKS

Jesus' life was an illustration of perfect communion with God. He interacted with His Father throughout the day, spent entire nights conversing with Him, and proclaimed He only did what the Father told Him to do. We can be sure Jesus experienced every struggle we face (Hebrews 2:10), and yet always remained within earshot of His Father. How can we hear as He did?

Put Aside Preconceptions

First, we must put aside preconceptions of what God's voice sounds like. We may miss God altogether because we expect Him to reveal himself in some majestic or mystical manner. One writer suggests that this happened to young Samuel when God called his name.

Samuel did not understand that the voice belonged to God, because it seemed so ordinary. He took it for Eli's voice, for surely the voice of God would be accompanied by awesome signs, by peals of thunder. Samuel's lack of experience was seen in his failure to realize that God does not speak in earsplitting declarations, but in subtle messages to the heart.[1]

Impressions of the Heart

This is how God speaks—in gentle impressions of the heart. As we wait in stillness and sense His presence, we are aware that a voice other than our own has joined our thoughts. Kelsey calls it "the voice of someone who cares about me, one who speaks to my deepest problems and fears, one who heals my wounds and restores my courage."[2]

God "comes right into our mind. Our thoughts are not only our thoughts; our desires are not only our desires—they may also be God's thoughts and desires. . . . He speaks secretly, noiselessly, as befits the Divinity."[3]

Francois Fenelon, martyred for his deep commitment to Jesus Christ in the late 1600s, encourages us to be silent in order to let God speak, and then "listen in the stillness of your heart."[4]

When we walk with God, taking the time to set our hearts aright before Him, we can be confident He will speak. As we still and quiet our souls, expecting Him to reveal himself, He responds. And when He does, we know we have heard Him.

Can you be mistaken about what you hear? Yes, and a later section examines this question. For now, believe in faith that you are His child, that He longs to be heard by you. As you turn your heart toward Him, know He has waited for this moment, knocking patiently at your soul's door, ready to commune in deep intimacy.

Listening Prayer can change you in wonderful ways. The God of the Universe is calling your name—can you hear Him? He wants to give himself completely to you—will you let Him?

Practicing Prayer: Getting to Know His Voice

Heart Preparation

Spend a few minutes thanking God for His presence and His willingness to speak. Affirm in faith that you are one of His sheep and therefore can know Him and hear His voice. Ask for His guidance as you pursue the subject of Listening Prayer.

Read 1 Samuel 3:1–11 and consider the following questions:

What was the situation concerning God's Word at this time? (v. 1).

What was true of Samuel concerning God's Word? (v. 7).

Why was Samuel living in this place? (See 1 Samuel 1:20–28.)

Where was Samuel when he first heard the voice? (v.3).

What does this represent? (See Exodus 25:22.)

What enabled Samuel to finally hear God's Word to Him? (vv. 10–11).

Although few heard God's voice during this time in history, God chose to speak to a boy who had no real experience of Him. Spend a few minutes looking at the conditions under which God spoke to Samuel. Is your life one that enables God to do the same?

- His life was completely dedicated to God.
- He resided in God's Presence.
- He placed himself as a servant under God's hand.
- He listened in faith.

Read the following verse aloud carefully: "Blessed is the man who listens to me, watching daily at my gates, waiting at my doorposts" (Proverbs 8:34). Rewrite this verse in your own words, personalizing it.

Write a short prayer describing your desires, your commitment, and your concerns to Jesus concerning learning to hear His voice in prayer.

DAY TWO: GOD'S PART

Every longing you have toward God is the result of His pursuing you. He wants to reveal himself, so He draws you gently to His side. He provides all that you need to hear Him. There are no mysteries or hidden clues on the road of Listening Prayer. It is as simple as two people getting to know each other. There is never a moment when this is not at the heart of our Gentle Shepherd.

He Is Present

E. Stanley Jones, missionary to India, had the opportunity of staying with Mahatma Gandhi for ten days. One day one of Gandhi's holy men asked Jones: "How can I find God?" Rev. Jones asked him to first share Ghandi's answer to the question. The man replied: "If you are going to find God, you must have as much patience as a man who sits by the seashore and takes up a drop of water at the end of a straw and thus empties the ocean."

Jones' answer was very different. He told the man: "I didn't find God—He found me. I turned around in repentance and faith, and I was in His arms. . . ."[5]

You don't have to find God. Turn and He is there. He is within you through His Spirit, and His presence permeates the air you breathe. You don't have to empty the ocean drop by drop, hoping when you finish He will decide to make himself known. If you come to Him with a seeking heart, like Nicodemus, He meets you. If you run in rebellion, like Jonah, He does not leave you. There is no place you can flee from His presence. (Psalm 139:7–12.)

This is important to Listening Prayer, because you are not at the mercy of an ambivalent God who may or may not show up to commune with you. Every second He stands ready to disclose himself. Like a child, just climb into His lap and wait. "Everybody rests at the end of the day; what a world gain if everybody could rest in the waiting arms of the Father, and listen until He whispers."[6]

He Reveals Truth

Do you ever feel like a laboratory mouse, looking for a way out of the maze concerning spiritual things? Trapped, you run into this wall and that, always moving, but never getting anywhere? Perhaps it even feels like God stands aloof, recording your progress for future experiments. Do not despair, for He can lift you from this endless entanglement and set you free. He isn't hiding His heart, nor do you have to strive to find it. His truth is revealed to any of His children who can hear it.

Jesus called the spirit that lives within us the *Spirit of truth* (John 14:16–17). God instructs us, feeds us, and quenches our spiritual thirst (Nehemiah 9:20). He reveals Jesus (John 15:26), guides us into all truth (John 16:13), and teaches us all things (John 14:26). We can come with confidence to God, for His Spirit is within us, accomplishing all He promised. This Spirit of truth is ready to speak—our choice to listen affirms this.

He Opens Our Ears

Beyond revealing truth, it is God's responsibility to make sure we understand it. We are utterly dependent upon His mercy to comprehend what He imparts. When God speaks and we try to absorb it with our finite minds, we miss His message. The one who delights in revealing his own mind instead of obtaining godly understanding is called a fool (Proverbs 18:2). He alone gives sight to our blinded eyes and sound to our deafened ears (Proverbs 20:12). We are enlightened with wisdom characterized by peace, mercy, and fruitful lives (James 3:17).

He Touches Our Deepest Soul

One agonizing day, King David was consumed with self-pity because of the success of wicked people all around him. Wanting to give up on God, he decided to go to the temple. There, he heard God's voice. He says, "When my heart was embittered, and I was pierced within, then I was senseless and ignorant; I was like a beast before Thee. Nevertheless I am continually with Thee; Thou hast taken hold of my right hand. With Thy counsel Thou wilt guide me" (Psalm 73:21–24).

Within each of us are longings, ambitions, fears, passions, and needs (of which we may not even be aware). God, who knows us better than we know ourselves, speaks in a way that touches our deepest parts. He uncovers sin, breaks down walls of pain, and peels off layer after layer of self protection until we are bare before Him. Then He does His greatest work.

In the presence of God, David saw the depths of his own despair and was broken over his bitterness. He held out his hand and received God's guidance. Listen to his heart afterward: "Whom have I in heaven but thee? And besides Thee, I desire nothing on earth. My flesh and my heart may fail; but God is the strength of my heart and my portion forever" (Psalm 73:25–26).

The inner prayer journey takes us along paths we've never pursued. God's purpose is to go deeper, touching all that keeps Him from accomplishing His perfect will for us. Through Listening Prayer, we open our minds and hearts for the cleansing, healing touch of our Master's hand.

This, then, is God's part in Listening Prayer: to be present, reveal truth, empower us to hear and understand, and to touch our deepest soul with His words. In the next session we will look at our part in Listening Prayer.

Practicing Prayer: God Speaks to You

Heart Preparation

Take some time to acclimate. Thank God out loud for His role in this part of the prayer journey: He is present, He reveals truth, He enables you to understand, and He touches your deepest soul. Spend a minute or two on each aspect, affirming its truth by faith and resting in Him.

Read Matthew 10:17–20, and Luke 12:11–12. Answer the following questions:

What promises are given here?

How will this be accomplished?

What does this say concerning Listening Prayer?

Read Isaiah 30:18–21. Answer the following questions:

What do we learn about God in verse 18?

What will bring us His blessing?

When will God answer? (verse 19).

How is God described in verse 20?

How will we hear His voice according to verse 21?

What are some areas in which you feel a need to hear God's voice?

Offer each of these things to the Lord. Affirm by faith that He will speak as you learn to listen in the coming days. Wait quietly in His presence and write down any thoughts you have in your prayer journal.

DAY THREE: MY PART

Listening Prayer is a joint venture between the creature and the Creator, the sheep and the Shepherd, the beloved and the Lover, the child and the Father. We have a part to play if we want to hear God's voice. We must learn to be still, to prepare our mind and heart, to listen and to respond.

Becoming Still

Every minute of the day our minds are flooded with the sounds of a society that has no interest in our spiritual condition. God seeks to break into this commotion with a fresh word. But how can we hear Him amidst all this clamor? "God is ever speaking, but even where there may be some inclination to hear, the sounds of earth are choking in our ears the sound of His voice."[7]

Sometimes we have to press through the upheaval without and within to become still. Elijah endured a mighty wind, an earthquake, and a great fire before God spoke in a still, small voice. We can't rush into God's presence, get a quick fix and run back to the whirlwind of our day. Stillness takes time.

> We must silence every creature, we must silence ourselves, to hear in the deep hush of the whole soul, the ineffable voice of the Spouse. We must bend the ear because it is a gentle and delicate voice, only heard by those who no longer hear anything else.[8]

When you stand perfectly still, your reflection is clear and bright in a pool of water. But even a small stone thrown into it makes it impossible to see anything. You need this kind of stillness. External noise must become a distant hum as you take every thought captive and put every longing of your heart to rest until the reflection in the pool is clear.

Preparing Our Heart and Mind

Once our soul is quiet and still, we prepare ourselves to listen. First, we call upon the Holy Spirit, for He alone gives life to the words we may hear. As we welcome Him, we acknowledge our dependency and inability to hear apart from His work.

Next, we remember who we are, and who God is. He made us for himself; it is His heart's desire to be in continual conversation with us. Charles Stanley says:

> Out of the billions of people who make up this universe, God is interested in you. He possesses intimate knowledge of you in His incomparable, indescribable mind. When you come to Him, you should draw near with a thankful heart, because you do not come in contact with a heavenly Father who speaks to the masses, but one who speaks to individuals.[9]

❧ ❧

Times of Dryness

At times, we may go through a period of dryness in our spiritual life, where it is difficult to sense God's presence. During these times, God is strengthening our faith—increasing our ability to serve Him because of who He is instead of what we may gain. By faith, we walk with Him, allowing Him to do this important work. We hold on to the truth He has given, clinging to His written Word regardless of what we feel. These times have been written about by profound spiritual leaders throughout history. (This Dark Night of the Soul will be examined more completely in Chapter 7.)

Prepare your heart with an attitude of anticipation. Turn your attention to Jesus, looking fully into the eyes of the One who gave His life. In waiting upon Him, your faith is established. This kind of expectancy does not come in the midst of hectic schedules and frantic movement. Faith comes by hearing, and you cannot hear unless you first prepare to listen.

Listening to His Voice

So often, our prayer lives are reduced to a grocery list—we check off each item we need and we're on our way. Then we can't understand why God doesn't speak. In order to listen, we must stop talking. We put aside our own agenda and ask God, *What do you have to say to me today?*

Tiny children scrutinize their mother or father's face. They watch for pleasure, anger, pride, or approval. Graham Kendrick, well-known modern hymn writer, says this is how he listens to God: "As a child learns to read his father's face for hundreds of silent messages, we can learn to look into God's face—to see what He wants, what His word to us is."[10]

Our ears are trained to listen to a nonstop chorus of television, radio, phone, kids, the neighbor's lawnmower, the garbage truck, traffic in the street, all these interfering with our ability to hear God. Like radios, we must be precisely tuned to receive His message. This process at first seems almost impossible. But through discipline and practice, we can learn to shut out the world in an instant, as our hearts expand under God's gentle voice.

Responding to God's Voice

Would you crawl out of bed in the morning, take a look at yourself in the mirror and then go to work, forgetting about your unkempt hair, sleep-filled eyes, and dirty face? God says we do this when we hear Him and do not respond. The voice of God always leaves us with choices. We may walk away, ignore Him, or fall on our face—but we make a choice every time He speaks.

Yet God does not make us listen, nor force us to respond. "As is evident from the history of the world, a characteristic of God is that God grants us the option to ignore. We need not heed the Divine."[11]

This is what makes our relationship with God so precious. He longs for us with supernatural passion, yet wants us to come to him on our own. He patiently draws us to His side and keeps us in the warmth of His embrace. How can we help but respond from our heart to this kind of love?

Practicing Prayer: The Still, Small Voice

Heart Preparation

Spend a few minutes becoming still in God's presence. Consciously release the cares of the day, tuning out the distractions within and without. Thank God that He loves you and desires to speak with you individually. Welcome His Holy Spirit as your guide into all truth. Open your ears to listen. Affirm that you will respond to what God reveals.

Read 1 Kings 19:1–13, Revelation 3:20.

Elijah had known both victory and despair and now wished he could just give up completely. But God was faithful to speak to Him. Today we will walk through his experience, gleaning truth for ourselves and hearing God's voice personally.

What things press in on you today?

What makes you long to run and hide?

Into Elijah's despair, a fierce wind blows, shattering great boulders with its force.

What would it be like to stand in the midst of this, wondering what God is trying to say?

Have there been times of turmoil like this in your life?

What is it like to see the hand of God but not hear His voice?

Then the earthquake.

What is it like to be uprooted, to lose your balance, your sense of direction?

What things bring you security?

God tears us from the familiar so we can learn to hear His voice. What is He breaking up in your life right now?

A fire ignites, rapidly spreading through the canyons of your life.

To what do you hold tightly, unable or unwilling to let go?

What would it take for you to be able to say, "Just as I am, without one plea . . ."?

Write down those things that keep you from falling barren before God's face.

Suddenly everything stops. There is silence. The wind has become a soothing breeze. Spend a few moments waiting in stillness before God. In the sound of a gentle whisper, God longs to share His heart.

What is He saying?

Take as long as you need. Once He has spoken, write it down. It might be words of comfort, conviction, or challenge. It may be a decision to make or a direction to go.

Respond to the voice of God as He leads.

Write significant lessons, truths, commitments, or impressions in your prayer journal.

DAY FOUR: HELP WITH HEARING GOD

God speaks to us in many ways. We may see His hand through circumstances, draw from the experience and counsel of other people, or discover principles of living from His Word. But Listening Prayer goes beyond seek-

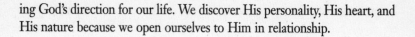

ing God's direction for our life. We discover His personality, His heart, and His nature because we open ourselves to Him in relationship.

Hearing God's Voice in His Word

Do you ever read the Bible and some verse you've heard for years springs to life? Turning it over and over in your heart like a precious jewel, you are pleasantly surprised to have such a thing in your possession. This is what happens when God speaks to us from His Word in Listening Prayer. The Spirit quickens the Word to our soul and we receive it in wonder.

Andrew Murray says the connection between the Word and prayer is one of the simplest lessons of the Christian life. "I pray—I speak to my Father; I read—my Father speaks to me."[12]

But how does God speak to us directly? How can His Word move from general inspiration to personal revelation? There is a very simple way to establish a habit of hearing God from His Word.

Stop—Look—Listen

First, open your Bible with a gentle spirit and quiet soul. Read slowly until something within urges you to STOP. Often only a word, phrase, or sentence has been read when this happens. Jeanne Marie Guyon, a French Christian in the 1600s wrote a book while imprisoned for her faith called *Experiencing the Depths of Jesus Christ*. In it she describes this process as "beholding the Lord." She says, "As you read, pause. The pause should be quite gentle. You have paused so that you may set your mind on the Spirit. You have set your mind inwardly—on Christ."[13]

Now, LOOK again at the words you have read and then to the face of God. Wait before Him, bringing all your attention to the indwelling Christ. Guyon continues, "Yes, by faith, hold your heart in the Lord's presence. Your attention is no longer on outward things or on the surface thoughts of your mind; instead, sweetly and silently, your mind becomes occupied with what you have read and by that touch of His presence."

When this has happened, we are ready to LISTEN. Our hearts are open as we quietly ask, "Lord, what do you have to say to me concerning this?" When God speaks we are forever changed. "It is to us the very voice of the Father, a real personal fellowship with himself. It is the living voice of God that enters the heart."[14]

Recently God spoke to me from a passage I could have overlooked. In Matthew 10, Jesus warns his disciples about the persecution they will face as they take the Gospel into the world. In verse 25, He says, "It is enough for the disciple that he become as his teacher, and the slave as his master." As I read, the Holy Spirit nudged me with the words "*It is enough.*"

I waited in God's presence, knowing He had something to say. I heard His gentle voice asking, *Is it enough? You are my slave . . . you are my disciple . . . is it enough for you to become like me?* He continued to ask, *Is it enough?* as I reflected on my spiritual journey. I saw all the things I wanted Him to do in me and for me, and realized none of it was as important as becoming like Him. Finally I responded, "Lord, I want to be like You more than anything, but so many things tend to cloud my vision."

God impressed upon me that He would ask this question many times in the coming days, but also that I was blessed and ready to receive a new measure of His grace and mercy. For many days I heard Him gently calling, *Is it enough?* This is just one example of the powerful experiences we can have as we come to God's Word in Listening Prayer.

Decision-Making and Listening Prayer

When we believe God has given us a specific word concerning some decision, there are a few questions that will help us make sure we are on the right track:

- *Does it fit with specific biblical mandates?*
- *Is it consistent with the whole of Scripture?*
- *Does it fit with the character of God as Scripture reveals?*
- *Have I sought godly counsel from other believers?*
- *Have I heard this consistently in the context of committing my life to Christ?*
- *Have I taken enough time to make sure this is what God is saying?*

Conversation With God

Jesus called us His friends, and friends know how to talk with each other. Prayer is a dialogue. We share—He listens. He speaks—we respond. Throughout Scripture God's people entered into conversation with Him, questioning, agreeing, wondering, clarifying, reacting, resisting, responding. When God speaks, He means for us to interact with Him—He made us this way.

One way to do this is to read Scripture and pray with a pen in hand. Listen and write down what you hear Him saying. Respond with your thoughts and wait for Him to speak again, writing it down when He does. You can pray through an entire book of the Bible this way, having a treasury of conversation with God to cherish throughout your spiritual journey.

Perhaps the best way to illustrate this is to give you a glimpse into one of my journals. For about nine months I sought to know God more by walking through Jesus' final days on earth. I spent most of the time in Listening Prayer. One day I heard Him speak from the cross: "*It is finished.*" Hushed and deeply stirred, I waited.

God spoke to me of His love, sharing that when He said, "*It is finished,*" He knew His children could finally understand how much He loved them. I pondered this, and was grieved at the way I had minimized the cross, judging those who wore crucifixes, proud that I served a risen Savior. I never understood how much it cost to show He loved me. I wrote:

> Lord—your love. How can I comprehend it? I know I have taken it lightly. This kind of love rocks me to my core, makes me want to be good enough—to make it worth your while. And yet if I could have done that, You wouldn't have had to come and die.
>
> I say, "I'm not worth it."
>
> I hear You saying, *You are.*
>
> I say, "You should never have done that."
>
> I hear You saying, *I did.*
>
> I say, "I'll make it up to You."
>
> I hear You saying, *Don't try.*
>
> I say, "What then? How can I live with this knowledge? It is too wonderful for me to attain."
>
> I hear You say, *Live in my love. It is for you I gave my life. I wanted you to know how much I care for you—how much I love you—to what lengths I would go to envelop you in my commitment to you. Try to learn to live in my love—this is all I ask.*
>
> I say, "I will Lord."

These are some simple ways to hear God in prayer. In the next section we will look at the difficulties we may encounter as we go deeper in our prayer journey by listening to God.

Practicing Prayer: On Your Own

Heart Preparation

Prepare your heart to hear God's voice by considering these questions:

Have I tuned out the distractions of my life to become still before God?

Have I called upon His Holy Spirit to guide and enlighten me with truth?

Have I remembered that it is God who wants to speak?

Do I expect to hear from Him?

Will I take the time to listen?

Will I respond as He leads?

Choose a passage from Scripture for this time of Listening Prayer. (The Gospels are a good place to begin.)

Stop. Hold your Bible open as you become still in His presence once again. Begin to read slowly, not for knowledge or understanding, but to hear God speaking. Do not try to analyze or interpret the verses. When you feel an urge to stop reading, pause. (If this doesn't happen, choose a portion that seems meaningful to you.)

Look. Read again the last few words, phrase, or sentence.

Set your mind on the indwelling Christ.

Turn all your focus toward Him as you ask, "Lord, what are you saying to me today?"

Listen. Wait quietly in His presence. If you do not get any impression from Him, slowly read the passage again and ask, "Lord, what are you saying to me today?"

Wait quietly, continuing to keep your focus completely on Him. If distracting thoughts come, let them go and return to the indwelling Christ.

When He speaks, either write it down or repeat it to yourself a few times.

If God leads, enter into a dialogue with Him concerning this. If not, thank Him for the word He has given.

Respond

Consider what difference this experience should make.

What is God telling you about your life?

How might you respond?

Write a response in your prayer journal. Be sure it includes thanksgiving.

DAY FIVE: DIFFICULTIES IN HEARING GOD

Henri Nouwen shows us that the Latin word *surdus*, from which *absurd* is taken, means *deaf*. To be deaf to God is to live in absurdity—never knowing when He calls or what direction He leads. Nouwen also points out that the Latin word for obey is *audire* which translates *all ears*. To obey God is to be *all ears to* His voice.[15]

Is your life absurd at times? Do you crave order and meaning? What would it take for you to be *all ears* toward God? He desires this and makes lavish overtures to you. But what stands in your way? Perhaps you hear Him for a while, and then His voice fades like a train in the distance. Why? There are several possibilities.

Paying the Price

It is difficult to be quiet long enough for God to speak. Our minds, jammed with signals from many frequencies, feel uneasy with silence, so we rush to fill its void. We can't get rid of this tendency by flitting here and there. Like a bee who penetrates the flower's depths, we must drink deeply of God's sweet nectar. To hear Him, we must pay the price of time. "Do not be hasty in word or impulsive in thought to bring up a matter in the presence

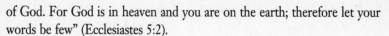

of God. For God is in heaven and you are on the earth; therefore let your words be few" (Ecclesiastes 5:2).

There is another price: selflessness. So often we come to God to promote our own agenda. We talk and talk and talk, reciting impotent prayers and crying out like sounding brass to a God we don't know very well. Instead, we must let God's perspective consume us until our tongue is silenced.

> What is the price of silence but the gift of self to God? It is to shut our eyes to what the world considers important and listen only to the Holy Spirit's call. . . . O how rare it is that the soul is sufficiently stilled to let God speak.[16]

The Door to Painful Issues

The silence that listening requires sometimes stirs things inside of us. One writer likens it to a dragnet effect, bringing up the good and the bad, the old and the new, the confusing and energizing inner issues of which we are not aware. This can be unsettling if we aren't aware that God is cleaning house. Personal purity is a difficult yet important by-product of Listening Prayer.

Through God's healing touch, we become aware of hurts we've hidden, weaknesses we've rationalized, and fears we've buried. Whatever is locked within the realms of our subconscious is fodder for the deep cleansing work of God. He is making us whole and as we listen, He opens the floodgate of our souls in the safety of His presence.

Sometimes we avoid silence because we fear this internal uprising; we suspect we have neglected inner issues and we would rather run. When God speaks, he pierces our self-protective armor. While this can be painful, it is also liberating. If we hold back to avoid the pain, we will never know the joy of hearing God. For the joy set before us, we endure the cross. This is an integral part of Listening Prayer.

Dealing With Troublesome Thoughts in Listening Prayer

1. Don't be discouraged or even shocked at your thoughts. God knew them before you and is not surprised.

2. Don't dwell on these thoughts or try to push them back down.

3. If sin is revealed, confess it, allowing God time to show you its source.

4. Let the thoughts go—gently release them into the Savior's hands. (See the chart on distracting thoughts in Chapter 1.)

5. Return quickly to God by affirming His presence; thank Him for His love and rest under His sheltering wings.

6. Declare your helplessness and desire to be whole. (Note: If you are plagued with obsessive thoughts during these times of quietness before God, and the above steps don't help, you may need to talk with your pastor or a Christian counselor.)

A Trained Ear

Have you ever watched a blind person when someone else enters the room? They listen intently, identifying the newcomer by his breathing, his gait or his movement. From birth, the blind train their ears to do for them what their eyes can't. We are spiritually blind—handicapped by our own sinful nature and the world's callous indifference to God. Without training, we won't hear God.

Listening Prayer is a discipline in which our ears become fine-tuned to the nuances of God's voice. This goes against our natural impulses. As Tozer says, we have "accepted the monstrous heresy that noise, size, activity, and bluster make a man dear to God."[17] This busyness of soul must be broken in the crucible of commitment. It doesn't go away because we wish it would.

I tend to treat God like I do my children. My eight-year-old will repeat something about three times before he screams at the top of his lungs, "Mom, you're not listening to me!!" My teenager used a different approach when he was small. He would grab my face, turn it to his and say, "What did I just say?" My ears have been trained to tune out the voices of those who mean the most to me. I wonder if God stands in heaven wanting to scream, *You're not listening to me!!* I feel Him turn my face toward His and ask, *What did I just say?*

Listening to God is not easy. We must practice, train, practice, train, and then practice and train some more. When we fail, we get up, brush the dust off and try again. When we struggle, we press on, knowing that through discipline we can persevere.

If you decided to learn to play the piano, would you take a few lessons and then quit because you couldn't play a concerto? Would a marine drop out of boot camp because he's tired and his feet hurt? Why should we expect God's training to require so little and produce so much? Don't give up on Listening Prayer. In time, with persistence and practice, it will become almost second-nature to you. It's worth the work.

The "O" Word

Obedience. No difficulty plagues us more in Listening Prayer than whether or not we will obey when God speaks. Obedience reflects a heart turned toward God. There is no other way to hear His voice. The prophets of old spewed out this message again and again:

- Zechariah mourned, "But they refused to pay attention, and turned a stubborn shoulder and stopped their ears from hearing. And they made their *hearts* like flint so that they could not hear the law and the words which the LORD of hosts had sent by His Spirit" (Zechariah 7:11–12, emphasis added).

- Jeremiah complained, "Behold, their ears are closed, and they cannot listen. Behold, the word of the LORD has become a reproach to them; they have no delight in it" (Jeremiah 6:10).
- God told Isaiah, "Go and tell this people: Keep on listening, but do not perceive; Keep on looking, but do not understand. Render the *hearts* of this people insensitive, their ears dull, and their eyes dim, lest they see with their eyes, hear with their ears, understand with their *hearts*, and repent and be healed" (Isaiah 6:10, emphasis added).

We must abandon ourselves to His purposes if we want to hear God. Otherwise, we may hear His words, and even enjoy them, yet be in great danger of deluding ourselves. God warned Ezekiel that He would destroy Jerusalem because of their rebellion, even though they listened to the prophet's words. He says: "Behold, you are to them like a sensual song by one who has a beautiful voice and plays well on an instrument; for they hear your words, but they do not practice them" (Ezekiel 33:32).

God speaks to everyone, but many don't hear. Their hearts, like flint, can absorb nothing, and soon the foundation of sand upon which they have built their lives will wash away, strewing debris in its wake. Jesus called this foolishness (Matthew 7:26). At this point in your inner prayer journey, what is the condition of your heart? You can go no further than the answer to this question.

Once we have made the watershed decision to surrender to God, He will provide an opportunity to demonstrate our commitment. When He speaks, we must ask: Will I obey? Do I want to? Can I pay the price? These are not easy questions; they strip away any pretense of faith.

When I first began my freelance writing career, I diligently followed every rule to find success. One speaker I heard instructed that publishers do not consider new writers unless they have a well-established speaking career. I attended some speaking seminars and prepared my promo sheet. But God had other plans.

One day as I shared my dreams with Him, I heard: *Let the speaking career go.* I started to argue, but His voice was so strong and clear, I knew the only thing left was my decision. Would I obey? This particular struggle was intense, but short, for long ago I gave God permission to do whatever He wanted with my writing. When He said, *Let the speaking career go*, I had to let it go.

Daily battles with obedience will be won only as we answer life's larger question: Whose life is this? It is His! To whom do I belong? I am His! He may have to remind me a thousand times a day, but I am His! The inner prayer journey establishes this over and over. When I am completely His, I am more concerned with submission than satisfaction, with abandonment than enjoyment, with obedience than success. These are the evidences of a hearing heart.

Is It His Voice?

Sometimes, we simply cannot seem to hear God speak, or we aren't sure that what we have heard is from Him. When this happens, the first thing we should do is ask ourselves some simple questions:

Am I taking enough time to really listen to God?

Have I let go of my own agenda in order to be open to His?

Am I allowing Him to purify me on a deep level?

Have I trained myself through discipline to hear God's voice?

Have I settled the larger question of whether I will obey when He speaks?

For most of us, dealing with these questions will give us what we need to hear God speak. But this is not an easy task. In fact, we should expect intense struggle as God seeks to conform us to the image of His Son. Jesus Christ struggled to the point of death and this is the example He calls us to follow (1 Peter 2:21). Through the agony of battle, we can only "[fix] our eyes on Jesus, the author and perfecter of our faith, who for the joy set before Him endured the cross" (Hebrews 12:2). In this, we will hear Him speak— clearly, lovingly, and compellingly.

Practicing Prayer: Working It Through

Heart Preparation

Spend a few minutes becoming acclimated to the presence of God. Welcome Him. See Him there with you, ready to speak. Ask Him to prepare the soil of your heart to hear exactly what you need today. Offer a sacrifice of praise for the times you have struggled with hearing His voice.

Today God will reveal the things that may keep you from hearing Him. Open your heart and mind, giving Him permission to show you anything He sees.

Prayerfully evaluate the following questions, allowing plenty of time for careful thought:

Am I taking enough time to really listen to God?

How much time do I regularly give to hearing God in prayer?

From His Word?

In my daily activities?

Have I let go of my own agenda in order to be open to His?

What do I want from God in prayer?

What might He be asking me to let go of?

What plans? Dreams? Ambitions?

What would it take for His plans to be my heart's passion?

Am I allowing His purifying work to be done in my deeper self?

Are there things I am afraid to have God open up within me?

Are there walls beyond which I don't want God to penetrate? Beyond which I don't even want to look?

Do I rush to cover anything God is gently revealing?

Do I believe His blood really pays the price for everything I have ever done or will do that brings shame to myself or to the name of Jesus?

Have I trained myself through discipline to hear God's voice?

How long have I been working at this part of the inner prayer journey?

Do I have expectations of success that discourage me when they aren't met?

Am I willing to keep trying even when I feel I've failed?

Will I trust God to accomplish His part?

Have I settled the larger question of whether I will obey when He speaks?

What is my answer to the question: Whose am I?

What does this mean on a daily basis?

Is there anything right now that would keep me from obeying God when He speaks?

Will I daily look to Him for strength to do His will?

Sit quietly with God. First, allow Him to gently reveal His love and commitment to You. Then, pour out your love to Him. Ask Him to share what He wants most from you right now. If He speaks, write it down. If He doesn't, assure Him you will keep asking until you know you have heard Him. Make this the cry of your heart for the next several days—in your prayer time and throughout your day: "Lord, what do you want from me or for me most right now?" Keep a journal of your thoughts, impressions, Scriptures, and answers from God concerning this issue.

Moving Forward

Listening Prayer changes us. You may want to spend a long time on this chapter. Learning to hear and obey the voice of God is crucial to everything else He wants to do in our lives, especially through the inner prayer journey. Take the time to learn of Him until His voice is so familiar you can't help but recognize it and respond.

We will go deeper in this process in the next chapter as we learn to evaluate the whole of our life in light of eternal perspectives. Through Recollective Prayer, we come to terms with our true values, priorities, and opportunities. It promises to be a challenging and eye-opening part of our inner prayer journey.

Notes

1. David J. Wolpe, *In Speech and In Silence: The Jewish Quest for God* (New York: H. Holt, 1992), pp. 152–153.
2. Morton T. Kelsey, *The Other Side of Silence* (New York: Paulist Press, 1976), p. 216.
3. Kilian J. Healy, *Walking With God* (New York: Declan X. McMullen Co., 1948), p. 35.
4. Francois Fenelon, *Christian Perfection* (New York: Harper & Row, 1941), p. 156.
5. E. Stanley Jones, *Song of Ascents* (Nashville: Abingdon Press, 1968), pp. 134–135.
6. Frank C. Laubach, *Letters by a Modern Mystic* (Old Tappan, N.J.: Fleming H. Revell Co., 1937), p. 62.
7. S. D. Gordon, *Quiet Talks on Prayer* (New York: Fleming H. Revell Co., 1941), p. 170.
8. Fenelon, pp. 155–156.
9. Charles Stanley, *How to Listen to God* (Nashville: Oliver-Nelson Books, 1985), p. 91.
10. Graham Kendrick, *Learning to Worship As a Way of Life* (Minneapolis: Bethany House, 1984), p. 174.
11. Wolpe, p. 153.

12. Andrew Murray, *With Christ in the School of Prayer* (Old Tappan, N.J.: Fleming H. Revell Company, 1972) p. 121.

13. Jeanne Guyon, *Experiencing the Depths of Jesus Christ* (Calif.: Goleta Books, 1975), pp. 10–11. (This book has been made available by various publishers. Check your local Christian bookstore for the current one.)

14. Murray, p. 124.

15. Henri Nouwen, *Making All Things New* (New York: Harper & Row, 1981) p. 68.

16. Fenelon, p. 156.

17. A. W. Tozer, *The Pursuit of God* (Camp Hill, Penn.: Christian Publications Inc., 1948), p. 80.

CHAPTER FIVE
RECOLLECTIVE PRAYER

Father, protect me from the onslaught of things,
both good and evil, that will bid my attention for this day.
Bob and Michael Benson

Imagine for a moment that you own a large jewelry store. It stocks both exquisite costume jewelry and the finest in genuine diamonds, silver, gold, and other precious stones. For years you have run the store with efficiency, taking some pride in the fact that it is always busy while other stores have fallen by the wayside.

But lately things aren't going so well. You're working harder than ever and people still flock to your store, yet your profits are shrinking. Unbeknownst to you, an angry employee has been switching price tags for months. A $2,000 diamond sells for $18.99 and a cubic zirconium for $3,200. A simple inventory check would reveal these things, but all you have time to do is keep the store running.

Many of our lives look uncomfortably like this jewelry store. Price tags are mixed up—we treasure worthless objects and sell our souls for pennies, but we're too busy to notice. So many things demand our attention that we have no choice but to continue day after day with business as usual. Unable to find a way to stop and take inventory, we end up spiritually, physically, and emotionally bankrupt.[1]

This is why we need Recollective Prayer. To recollect is to "call to mind, remember, gather again; to regain control of oneself, one's thoughts."[2]

In Recollective Prayer, we bring our lives before God to gain perspective, guidance, and direction. "It is a matter of daily, hourly going down into the Shekinah of the soul, in that silence, find yourselves continually recreated, and realigned and corrected again and again from warping effects of outer affairs."[3]

No people have faced a greater need for this kind of prayer than today's Christian. Technology demands that we continually move, change, and re-negotiate reality, or be left behind. Our lifestyle simply does not lend itself to quiet times of reflection and reorientation.

Yet it is precisely these times that must become the great need and habit of our hearts. We have to close the store and take the time to check our stock list. Have the tags gotten mixed up? What are our priorities? What value are we placing on the pieces of our lives?

Without a commitment to regular times of prayerful reflection, we will always be caught up in the whirlwind of our chaotic existence. We may have the best of intentions, but the pull of life's demands makes us slaves to the urgent and masters of nothing. Under God's hand, we need to regain control, spiritually regroup, and gather the pieces of our lives together on a regular basis. This is Recollective Prayer.

DAY ONE: YOUR OWN JEWELRY STORE

What jewels adorn the display cabinets of your life? I think of a little brown-skinned boy who zips through my days with energy and enthusiasm that often exhausts me. He is a gift—God handed him to us when we had lost hope of ever having more children.

Then there is the blond boy-man who I must watch from a distance as he handles his first year of college. I have friends who pray with me, laugh with me, and hold me accountable. My companion-husband's warm eyes and familiar touch bring joy to my daily existence. And the Lover of my soul—my Lily of the Valley—my Savior, shines like the morning star through the days and nights of my life. These are some of my precious stones. What are yours?

Even as I wax nostalgic over these things, I am confronted with the harsh reality that I don't always value them for what they are worth. I rush my little one to bed, ignoring his meandering conversation so I can read the newspaper or watch TV. I snap at my teenager in a tone I wouldn't use with a stranger. I neglect friends and take my husband for granted. When I stop and reflect, my heart is heavy and I vow to change things. It is something I must do often.

Through Recollective Prayer, we consider our past, present, and future in the process of spiritually gathering ourselves together. Eugene Peterson reminds us, "We need roots in the past to give obedience ballast and breadth; we need a vision of the future to give obedience direction and goal. And they must be connected. There must be an organic unity between them."[4]

The Past

Sometimes our lives look like a board game where we keep drawing the *go back to start* card. Without knowledge and insight from our past, we make the same mistakes, fall into the same sinful patterns, and waste a lot of time. There is purpose in putting our past in perspective.

The Present

God never intended for His people to relegate Him to weekly worship or periodic prayers. He wants to permeate the present of our lives. The only way we can aspire to such serious spirituality is by checking in every day and throughout the day with the Lord who is our Shepherd. If we let one or two or three days go by, we lose the opportunity to make the simplest kinds of changes. Habits form, commitments control, and we can't find a way out of the hubbub. We will always find relief by coming back to our Source, but how much easier if we had come sooner and more often.

The Future

We are a people who live by faith, and faith is "the assurance of things hoped for, the conviction of things not seen" (Hebrews 11:1). How do we know what to hope for? How can we be sure of what we do not see? We come before God, allowing His words to give form to our future, and foot leather to our dreams. He opens our eyes and shows us where we are going, invigorating us with vision.

Putting Them Together

In Recollective Prayer, the pieces of the puzzle fall into place in the light of God's loving guidance. Like a common thread woven through an intricate design, we see His hand. Our past gives us perspective, our present pulls us to His side, and our future forces us to walk by faith. This can be a rejuvenating part of the inner prayer journey. Will you open your life to the gentle intervention of Almighty God?

Practicing Prayer: Taking Inventory

Heart Preparation

Take some time to focus your mind on spiritual things. Read Psalm 84 aloud, meditatively as a prayer from you to God. Ask the Holy Spirit to guide you during this time. Invite God to reveal anything that hinders Him from working as He wants to in your life.

Picture in your mind the jewelry store of your life. First, list everything in it—the things that have great value and those that don't. (Include relationships, spiritual life, possessions, vocation, time usage, talents, abilities, etc.)

Now prayerfully examine your list by asking the following questions:

- What is of real value and what is an imitation?
- What do I hold up, polish, cherish, and take the time to keep shining?
- Which jewels have lost their value?
- Which jewels are on a shelf, covered with dust and unused, that God wants to clean and polish and give their rightful value?
- What might others see when they look in the window of my store?

Read Matthew 6:19–21. According to verse 21, where is our heart? Based on the spiritual inventory you have just done, where is *your* heart? Write out a prayer based on your thoughts and impressions from God. It may be repentance, thanksgiving, a cry for help, or something else (or all of these). Offer it to God, asking for His will as you continue on this part of the inner prayer journey.

DAY TWO: GOD'S WORD

One day the teenage prophet Jeremiah faced a future full of despair. He lamented bitterly, "My strength has perished, and so has my hope from the LORD." But as he waited before God, his heart began to change.

He looked at his past and said, "This I recall to my mind, therefore I have hope. The LORD's lovingkindnesses indeed never cease, for His compassions never fail."

He looked to the day at hand and added, "They are new every morning."

Then the future took on fresh meaning as He concluded, "The LORD is my portion, therefore I have hope in Him" (Lamentations 3:18, 21–24).

This is the kind of Recollective Prayer we see throughout Scripture. The book of Psalms records many of these intimate conversations between David and God. Holding up the pieces of his life, David reflects:

"Examine me, O LORD, and try me; Test my mind and my heart . . ." (Psalm 26:2).

"Teach me Thy way, O LORD, and lead me in a level path . . ." (Psalm 27:11).

"Create in me a clean heart, O God, and renew a steadfast spirit within me" (Psalm 51:10).

Jesus' model prayer is one of recollection. He teaches:

- For yesterday: Ask for forgiveness and the strength to forgive others.
- For today: Seek God for the simplest needs you have.
- For tomorrow: Pray for guidance and deliverance.

The Bible and the Past

The word *remember* is woven throughout the pages of biblical history. The prophets warned God's people to *remember* how God had worked in the past. "Remember the former things long past, for I am God, and there is no other; I am God, and there is no one like Me, declaring the end from the beginning . . ." (Isaiah 46:9–10). David said: "I remember the days of old; I meditate on all Thy doings" (Psalm 143:5).

Perhaps the keenest admonitions to the early church were given to John on the Isle of Patmos. The church at Ephesus was called to remember their first love, while the church at Sardis was challenged to remember the things they had been taught (Revelation 2:4–5; 3:3). We can judge our life in Christ today by looking back to where we once were.

The Bible and Our Present

Every day we live has a purpose in the scheme of eternity. Life is a vapor and we have no idea what tomorrow may hold (James 4:14). David wrote an entire Psalm about this. "As for the days of our life, they contain seventy years, or if due to strength, eighty years, yet their pride is but labor and sorrow; for soon it is gone and we fly away." Then he offers a plea in light of this understanding: "So teach us to number our days, that we may present to Thee a heart of wisdom" (Psalm 90:10, 12).

This is the only life we have—our only chance to impact eternity. Today does make a difference. God calls us to acknowledge Him in all our ways (Proverbs 3:6) and we do this by offering him this moment, this day, to use as He wills.

The Bible and Our Future

God wants us to plan for the future. He tells us to learn from the ant who prepares its food in the summer and gathers its provision in the harvest (Proverbs 6:6–8). But we are always to do this in the context of His wisdom and guidance. "I know, O LORD, that a man's way is not in himself; Nor is it in a man who walks to direct his steps" (Jeremiah 10:23). "Commit your works to the LORD, and your plans will be established" (Proverbs 16:3).

God sent young Joseph his dreams and Abraham the night sky object lesson so they would hold on to the future He had for them. Abraham could walk up a mountain ready to sacrifice his own son because he lived in the light of the promise God had given. Joseph remembered his dreams and was able to say to his brothers: "Do not be grieved or angry with yourselves, because you sold me here; for God sent me before you to preserve life" (Genesis 45:5).

There is great encouragement in receiving vision for our future directly from the God of the Universe who promises: "For I know the plans that I have for you, plans for welfare and not for calamity to give you a future and a hope" (Jeremiah 29:11).

Practicing Prayer: Checking It Out Yourself

Heart Preparation

Take some time to thank God for His hand in your life—in the past, the present, and the future. Sing or speak the words of the following hymn as a prayer of commitment:

> *Take my life and let it be*
> *Consecrated Lord to Thee;*
> *Take my hands and let them move*
> *At the impulse of Thy love,*
> *At the impulse of Thy love.*
>
> *Take my feet and let them be*
> *Swift and beautiful for Thee;*
> *Take my voice and let me sing*
> *Always, only, for my King,*
> *Always, only, for my King.*
>
> *Take my lips and let them be*
> *Filled with messages for Thee;*
> *Take my silver and my gold—*
> *Not a mite would I withhold,*
> *Not a mite would I withhold.*

Take my love—my God, I pour
At Thy feet its treasure store;
Take myself—and I will be
Ever, only, all for Thee,
Ever, only, all for Thee.[5]

Ask God to guide your thoughts as you come before Him today.

Read Revelation 2:1–6 and 3:1–3.

What was each church like according to these verses (Ephesus and Sardis)?

In each case, why are they instructed to look at their past?

When you think of your spiritual life, what are some reasons God might want you to look at your past?

Read Psalm 90:1–6, 10–12.

From God's perspective, what does our life look like?

How does an understanding of the brevity of your own life affect you spiritually?

What do you think it means to *number our days?*

Read Hebrews 11:6–19. Consider Noah and Abraham and answer the following questions about each one:

How did they know what their future would hold?

How did they demonstrate faith in what God had said?

What was the result of their obedience?

In what ways does your life give testimony to trusting God for your future?

Spend some time gathering your thoughts together in God's presence. Bring your life before him, waiting on His voice to give clarity and perspective. Write a prayer of commitment concerning this part of your prayer journey.

DAY THREE: DAILY RECOLLECTION

Plan Your Path

Praying over the details of your day is a great time-management program. Remember the jewelry store? A quick perusal of the merchandise could have saved the owner a lot of money and headache. This process is really one of quality control. The quality of our lives is at stake—isn't it worth a few minutes a day?

When you first awake, or as part of your normal quiet time, take about five minutes to offer your day to the Lord. Pray through your schedule—sometimes it helps to have your calendar in hand.

Open yourself completely to the guidance of the Lord, giving Him permission to change your plans. Once you have set your priorities according to spiritual wisdom, you will accomplish the most important things. Always be aware however, that if and when things don't go as planned, God is still sovereign and not surprised at all by circumstances that change.

Practice His Presence

How do we hold on to the commitment we made earlier, when our day begins to feel like a pressure cooker? Brother Lawrence, a priest whose ministry involved mundane chores, such as cooking and housework, offers us a simple answer: *Practice the presence of God*. Listen to his words:

> We might accustom ourselves to a continual conversation with Him, with freedom and in simplicity . . . that we need only to recognize God intimately present with us, to address ourselves to Him every moment, that we may beg His assistance for knowing His will in things doubtful, and for rightly performing those that we plainly

see He requires of us, offering them to Him before we do them, and giving thanks when we have done.[6]

Brother Lawrence outwardly washed dishes, while he inwardly communed with God. As we grow in discipline and desire, our minds can learn to operate on two levels at once. One level is the mental process it takes to handle external affairs. But, almost like a "behind the scenes" drama, we can be in prayer, worship, and attentive listening to the voice of God. Our goal is to learn to do this more and more, increasing our ability to maintain this deeper level.

Jesus taught that if we learn to be faithful in little things, we will be faithful in great things. The minutiae of daily life is as small as it gets and finding God in the details is a struggle. Brother Lawrence tells of profound inadequacy and disappointing failure, but by constantly renewing his commitment he came to a point where he could not conceive of God ever being away from His thoughts.

Ponder the Past

In the quiet moments just before you fall asleep at night, take some time to think about your day. Ponder your activities and the people you encountered. Enter into a dialogue with God about these things. This usually need take no more than five minutes and is a wonderful way to fall asleep with spiritual focus.

Daily Recollection in a Nutshell

Plan Your Path: (in the morning)

- *Lord, is there anything I am planning to do that isn't according to Your will?*

- *Is there any wisdom You want to give concerning people, places, or events ahead?*
- *Are there things I should add that aren't on my schedule?*

   Practice His Presence: (through the day)

- *Seek His guidance on current situations.*
- *Release words of love and adoration.*
- *Listen for His voice.*
- *Sing a short song of praise.*
- *Offer the work you are doing to Him.*

   Ponder the Past: (before bed)

- *Was my day pleasing to You?*
- *Is there anything I should have done differently?*
- *Were there any occasions of sin?*
- *Were You trying to speak to me in some way I missed?*

Practicing Prayer: Day by Day

Heart Preparation

This devotional process will take place in three parts. Ask God to guide you, strengthen your resolve, and make His presence known in a new way through these times. Use the chart above for the exercise.

In the Morning: Set a goal to spend a few minutes for the next three mornings offering your day to the Lord. Lay out your schedule before Him, asking the questions from the chart under *Plan Your Path*.

Once you have done this, affirm in faith that this is the day the Lord has made and that you will trust Him with all the details of it. Keep a log of your experiences in your prayer journal.

After a few days, consider the following questions:

How have my days differed as a result of this part of Recollective Prayer?

How have I seen God's hand in a way I might have missed had I not done this?

Write your thoughts in your journal.

Throughout the Day: Commit to the art of practicing God's presence by setting a reasonable goal for yourself. Perhaps you will decide to touch base with Him three times during your day at first. The important thing is to choose specific times you will do this each day. (For example, each time you are in the car, before each meal, before certain activities, etc.)

You may want to jot down the things in the chart under *Practice His Presence* on a 3×5 card to carry with you. After a few days, consider:

Do I feel successful at practicing God's presence?

Am I doing this more than before?

What difference does practicing God's presence make in my day?

Before You Go to Sleep: For the next few days, commit to praying just before you go to sleep, asking the questions from the chart on *Ponder the Past*

After a few days, consider the following:

How has this nighttime practice of Recollective Prayer impacted me throughout the day?

What are some hindrances to doing this every night?

Why would I want to make this a regular part of my spiritual life?

Be sure to keep a journal of your experiences with daily Recollective Prayer.

DAY FOUR: PERIODIC RECOLLECTION

A biologist once went to Africa to study forms of life found deep in the jungle. He hired a group of native men to help carry his equipment, and on the first day they made great progress. The scientist was pleased, but when he rose early the next morning the men were all sitting quietly, refusing to move. When he asked the interpreter what was wrong, he responded, "The men say they went too fast and hard yesterday. Now today they must wait for their souls to catch up with their bodies."

Sometimes we need to wait for our *souls* to catch up. We must slow it all down—our activities, responsibilities, relationships, and thought processes until we possess a quietness that allows us to be renewed and refreshed. This is the purpose of periodic Recollective Prayer. It can be done monthly or several times a year and takes at least an hour of uninterrupted time.

Review the Past

Here, we evaluate our spiritual growth, looking at all the parts of our life. We tend to compartmentalize things and only let God in on those things we consider "spiritual". To Him, everything is spiritual—the way we treat our spouses and children, our integrity in the workforce, the quality of our labor, the use of our time—all these things and more should be part of Recollective Prayer.

Realign Today's Priorities

My husband, who suffers from a curved spine, occasionally needs chiropractic care. Usually he puts off going until his back pain is unbearable and his shoulders are like rocks from tension. After one hour of treatment, his face is relaxed and his body free from pain. Apparently, the chiropractor adjusts his spine until it is aligned properly.

This is what we want to do on a spiritual level through Recollective Prayer. We peruse our priorities, tossing things out, keeping those that are still important, and adding new things until we are aligned with God's will.

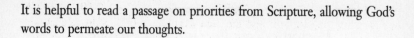

It is helpful to read a passage on priorities from Scripture, allowing God's words to permeate our thoughts.

Bible Passages on Priorities

Matthew 6:19–34 • Matthew 13:43–46 • 1 Timothy 6:10–19 •
Luke 10:38–42 • Matthew 16:24–27 • Philippians 3:7–10 •
1 Peter 1:13–25 • 2 Corinthians 4:16–5:10 • Luke 12:15–21

Renewing our Vision

Finally, we bring all that we know of the coming weeks to God in prayer, asking for specific guidance and divine involvement. This may involve changes in things such as career, family situation, living arrangements, ministry positions, etc. We take the time to listen to God concerning these things.

When God guides, we walk with confidence and expectation. There is no limit to our dreams and visions for the future. Eugene Peterson calls it "imagination put in the harness of faith."[7]

We know that God will fulfill His plans and purposes in His way and time. Nothing can propel us forward in spiritual growth like this.

Periodic Recollection at a Glance

Review the Past:

- *Lord, in what areas have You been seeking to discipline and teach me?*
- *What mistakes have I made?*
- *Have I hurt others?*
- *Have I demonstrated Your love and compassion?*
- *What have I done which is pleasing to You?*
- *Where has growth taken place?*
- *Are there any areas where I'm stuck?*

Realign Today's Priorities:

- *Lord, what can I eliminate from my life?*
- *In what ways do I waste time?*
- *What am I not doing that I should be doing?*
- *In what order of priority are the parts of my life?*
- *In what order should they be?*

Renew Your Vision:

- *Lord, what do you want to do within me in the next few weeks?*
- *How do you want to improve my relationships with others?*
- *Should I be considering any changes in my life?*
- *Are you calling me to something new?*

Practicing Prayer: A Mini-Retreat

Heart Preparation

Choose a time in the next week for extended Recollective Prayer. You will need at least an hour free from distractions and interruptions. You may want to go to a park, the beach, etc., to get away from the phone and home or work responsibilities. Ask God to begin preparing your heart to hear as you approach this special time.

When you are ready to begin, spend a few minutes in quiet prayer, offering the time to God. Read aloud from the Psalms, or sing a simple praise song. Take a few minutes to breathe out distractions and breathe in God's presence (see Chapter 1).

Open your prayer journal and/or your calendar. Skim the past few weeks entries and begin to thank God specifically for answered prayer and other blessings. As you thank Him, let your heart be drawn toward Him in worship and adoration. You may want to write some words of gratitude in your prayer journal.

Write a list of the components of your life: Work, family, other relationships, church ministry, community involvement, neighborhood, etc. As you look at this list, offer the questions from the chart above under *Review the Past*.

Read Matthew 6:19–34 slowly and prayerfully. In light of these truths, seek to evaluate the questions from the chart under *Realign Today's Priorities*.

Make sure to consider your devotional life—what place does it have? What do you need to do to make sure this is given the right priority? Picture the pieces of your life perfectly aligned as God wills them to be. Ask Him to make this a reality in the coming days.

Read Proverbs 3:5–6. Be completely open to God's Spirit, giving Him your undivided attention and willingness to listen. Be ready for Him to surprise you with new dreams and fresh vision.

Now look forward to the coming weeks. You may want to jot down the key events or commitments you have. Bring each of these to the Lord, asking the questions from the chart under *Renew Your Vision*.

End this time with thanksgiving and commitment. Look back over your notes and thank God for what He has done today. Praise Him for His intimate concern with the details of your life. Commit yourself to walk in obedience in the power of His Spirit.

DAY FIVE: ANNUAL RECOLLECTION

Once a year we need to find several hours in which God can have our undivided attention. This is the purpose of annual Recollective Prayer. For a day or two we focus exclusively on our relationship to God. Freed from normal responsibilities and away from interruptions, incredible things can happen.

Remembering the Past

My life consists of many pieces in various sizes, shapes, and colors. Thrown into a bag and pulled out one by one, they don't make much sense— just a jumbled mess of ups and downs, joys and sorrows, excitement and monotony, growth and setbacks. But when I lay them out in order, a story begins to emerge. I have a history, and woven through each page is the hand of a compassionate God who planned for my existence long before my first breath.

Paul Tournier notes that until we stop and look back, we won't realize the degree to which God is involved in our lives.

> Only afterward, as we look back over the way we have come and reconsider certain important moments in our lives in the light of all that has followed them, or when we survey the whole progress of our lives, do we experience the feeling of having been led without knowing it, the feeling that God has mysteriously guided us.[8]

We gain perspective as our emotion-driven beliefs crumble in the light of all God has done. Eugene Peterson reminds us that "Christian disciple-ship is . . . making a map of the faithfulness of God, not charting the rise and fall of our enthusiasms."[9]

Today we may not see God's hand, but we persevere because we remember the extent of His involvement in all the parts of our history.

Reevaluate Today's Priorities

Stradivari of Cremona, the famous maker of violins, is said to have marked every violin he made with the name of Jesus. Today his incredible work is still called *Stradivarius del Gesu*. Wouldn't you love everything in your life to bear the mark of Jesus—to leave a heritage like Stradivari did, which continues to give living testimony of our Lord?

Through annual recollection, we place the pieces of our life under the light of Scripture. We might read one of the Gospels, jotting down words Jesus said, focus on the parables of Jesus, noting the recurrent themes, or quickly peruse Paul's letters, jotting down issues related to our situation, as we evaluate what mark we are leaving on the things we touch.

Recreate for the Future

A sign that hung in my college library said, *If you don't know where you're going, you'll probably end up somewhere else*. Without a plan, we either drift aimlessly or are pulled in the direction of the strongest force. We end up discouraged, burned out, cynical, or exhausted.

God has a plan and He longs to reveal it to us. Have you asked Him lately what His plan is for your life? The exciting thing about God's plan is that it rejuvenates. Burnout doesn't occur when we allow God to be our daily guide on life's journey. (This doesn't mean we won't be tired, disappointed, or discouraged, but we can find strength in the confidence that God is fulfilling His plan in His way).

In annual Recollective Prayer, we dream big dreams by opening ourselves to all the possibilities that are available to us as His children. God loves to work with people in this way. Sarah laughed heartily at God's idea to give her a child at age ninety, but that's exactly what God did. "Why did Sarah laugh. . . ?" He asked. "Is anything too difficult for the LORD?" (Genesis 18:13–14).

I went through this process last year as God called me to pray for my oldest son, who was leaving for college. I sensed that this could be the year he developed a passion for God. Since then, I have prayed for my son regularly and shared with him about my own relationship with God during my college days. I have also learned that I must let go if he questions my values, rejects them, or struggles to find his own. My trust is in God's faithfulness—nothing is too difficult for Him.

<hr />

A Silent Retreat

Many Christian retreat centers now offer silent retreats where meals are provided, but otherwise you are left on your own. Strict silence is observed as each person charts their personal retreat in the beauty of that special place. These exercises are excellent for a silent retreat.

<hr />

Practicing Prayer: Annual Recollection—Getting Away From It All

Heart Preparation

Make plans for this getaway. Choose a place where you will be free from distractions and interruptions. If you plan to stay home, unplug the phones and put a *do not disturb* sign on your door. You will need at least one whole day (six to eight hours). It is ideal to have two days to provide for breaks, etc., but not necessary. Prior to the getaway, read through the exercises in order to prepare your mind and heart.

Begin your time reading aloud from the Psalms, singing some praise and worship songs. and thanking God for His presence in your life. Offer yourself to Him for these hours, asking His Spirit to guide and empower you.

Remembering the Past: Spend some time reviewing your life, including this year. Write down the major, significant events, important periods, and other things that are pertinent. Beneath each one, write how God's hand was in it, the lessons you have learned, and the blessings you have received. You can skip this process if you have done it recently. (Create a chart like the one below.)

In what ways are you encouraged through this process?

What things are you still waiting on God to understand or see fulfilled?

Spend some time in thanksgiving. Be specific. Write a prayer of response.

Take a break before you begin the next section. Go for a walk, take a swim, eat something, stretch, etc. You may want to rest, listening to some instrumental music.

Reevaluate Today's Priorities: Choose one of the Gospels to read at least twice. First, read it from beginning to end as if it were a story you've never read (If you have a *Living Bible* or *The Message*, read from it.)

Now read again, slowly. Jot down words that Jesus spoke concerning lifestyle and priorities. When you are finished, prayerfully review what you have written.

Consider these questions concerning your life in light of what you've read:

Who am I?

Why am I here?

What is my calling in life?

How am I living up to it?

How serious am I about the commitments Jesus calls me to?

How do the choices I am making fit with what God desires of me?

Based on this time, write a covenant with God concerning changes you want to make. Be specific. Think of who you could share this with in the coming days.

Take another break before beginning the next section. It may be time to eat a meal, take a nap, or just rest. Don't try to fill your mind with reading, unless it is something light and uplifting.

Recreate for the Future: Read the story of Abraham in Genesis 15:1–6; 18:1–14; 21:1–5. Think of your own life in light of the obstacles Abraham faced concerning his future. Hear God's voice asking you, *Is anything too difficult for me?*

Look to the year ahead of you. Open your mind to possibilities in all areas of your life. Write down the categories: personal, spouse, children, career, ministry, extended family, education, etc. Dream big—if you could see anything happen in each of them, what would it be?

Pray through each, asking the following questions:

Lord, might this be your will?

Is there anything in this that is displeasing to you?

Are my motives for your glory or my own pleasure?

Am I dreaming big enough?

Now start a new list, writing only those things you feel confident God is guiding you in. You are seeking to know His will; you don't have to know all the details. If you are unsure, write it down with a question mark beside it.

Offer the list to God, asking Him what steps you need to take to make them happen. Be careful not to make things work by your own efforts. God

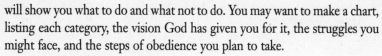

will show you what to do and what not to do. You may want to make a chart, listing each category, the vision God has given you for it, the struggles you might face, and the steps of obedience you plan to take.

Memorize Ephesians 3:20–21:

> Now to Him who is able to do exceedingly abundantly beyond all that we ask or think, according to the power that works within us, to Him be the glory in the church and in Christ Jesus to all generations forever and ever. Amen.

Finally, praise God in advance for all He will do. Worship Him for who He is, what He has done and what He will do. Affirm your commitment to follow Him in faith.

Moving Forward

Recollective Prayer is like tuning an engine. If it is done regularly, all the parts will run smoothly. Without it, little things break down and before we know it the engine is useless. This tool can keep us on the narrow road through our inner prayer journey.

In the next chapter, we will look more deeply at the priorities and commitments our lives hold. In a world whose values are in stark contrast to the teachings of our Lord, how can we stay focused? How do we keep our hearts pure from the corruption of consumerism? How do we live as believers in the context of a fallen world? We will discover the answers to these tough questions as we learn to pray the Prayer of Detachment.

Notes

1. My thanks to Morton Kelsey for briefly passing on this thought in his book, *The Other Side of Silence*, (New York: Paulist Press, 1976), p. 92.

2. *The New Lexicon Webster's Dictionary of the English Language* (New York: Lexicon Publications, 1989), p. 833.
3. Thomas Kelly, *The Eternal Promise* (New York: Harper & Row, 1966), p. 105.
4. Eugene H. Peterson, *A Long Obedience in the Same Direction*, (Downers Grove, Ill.: InterVarsity Press, 1980), pp. 165–166.
5. Words by Frances Havergal, Music by Henri A. Cesar Malan, Public Domain.
6. Brother Lawrence, *Practicing the Presence of God* (Old Tappan, N.J.: Fleming Revell Co., 1969), p. 23.
7. Peterson, p. 140.
8. Paul Tournier, as quoted in Bob & Michael Benson, *Disciplines of the Inner Life* (Nashville: Generoux, 1989), p. 223.
9. Peterson, p. 129.

CHAPTER SIX
THE PRAYER OF DETACHMENT

O world, so frail and so mad! Is it you in which we are made to believe? You are only a dream, and you want us to believe in you! . . . Are you not ashamed to give magnificent names to the showy miseries by which you dazzle those who are attached to you?

Francois Fenelon (A.D. 1651–1715)

I didn't want to write this chapter—to lay out lessons never learned or commitments never kept. While it needed to be written, I wondered how to speak with integrity from the setbacks and roadblocks in my own life. One day I pleaded with God, "Father, I don't know how to be in the world but not of it, to crush the idols of greed and materialism that command my allegiance. I read of others who do, and my heart yearns to love you that much. My spirit is willing but my flesh is so very weak."

God hears desperate cries. Through His Word, He showed me that my heart was hard and rocky soil. He promised He would plow and furrow and nourish it until eternal seeds could take root. Today tiny buds of growth surprise and humble me. So while every word of this book reflects my personal journey, this chapter in particular bears the scars of my struggle, the still tender wounds and the fresh tracks of a battle long overdue.

This chapter could be called *The Prayer of Attachment*, for an ascetic detachment from the things of the world by itself holds no real spiritual value. What we need is wholehearted attachment to our living Lord. Jesus said: "You shall love the LORD your God with all your heart, and with all your soul, and with all your mind." (Matthew 22:37). As our hearts are bound to Jesus Christ, the world's temporal treasures lose their appeal.

However, Jesus knew how easily we would lose sight of this and slip into loyalties having nothing to do with faith. He talked of this subject with deep concern:

> For where your treasure is, there will your heart be also (Matthew 6:21).
>
> And the one on whom seed was sown among the thorns, this is the man who hears the word, and the worry of the world, and the deceitfulness of riches choke the word, and it becomes unfruitful (Matthew 13:22).
>
> For what will a man be profited, if he gains the whole world, and forfeits his soul? (Matthew 16:26).
>
> You fool! This very night your soul is required of you; and now who will own what you have prepared? (Luke 12:20).
>
> Be on guard, that your hearts may not be weighted down with . . . the worries of life, and that day come on you suddenly like a trap (Luke 21:34).

How do we embrace such difficult words? How can we live the teachings of Christ when everything around us screams something else? Our culture's values of success, accumulation, prosperity, and power have seeped into the Christian consciousness until it is difficult to distinguish God's people from anyone else. Every day is a struggle to ferret the truth from the plethora of messages hurled our way.

The Prayer of Detachment is a plea for passionate *attachment* to God and His reality. As Brennan Manning poignantly asks, "How do we build

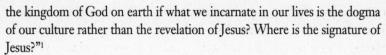

the kingdom of God on earth if what we incarnate in our lives is the dogma of our culture rather than the revelation of Jesus? Where is the signature of Jesus?"[1]

If you want the signature of Jesus engraved on your heart, it requires drastic change. You will find no contentment until you "throw yourself into His bosom, and come to His heart, to God's very heart."[2]

In coming to the heart of God, we find everything we have longed for in a world void of eternal treasure. Fenelon reminds us:

> For it is in seeing God that we see the nothingness of the world, which will vanish in a little while like smoke. All the grandeurs, and their paraphernalia, will flee away like a dream. . . . Where have they gone? we shall say. Where are those things that have charmed our hearts?[3]

It takes courage to open the hidden hollows of our heart and discover what prevents wholehearted devotion to Jesus Christ. It may be a lonely process causing us to cry out: "Come Lord Jesus!" Perhaps you have heard eternity calling lately. Will you answer its distant whisper?

DAY ONE: PUTTING IT IN PERSPECTIVE

What draws you to the Prayer of Detachment? Do you sense a growing discomfort with things as they are? When your heart touches eternity's gates, do you long to hold it closer . . . longer?

Many religions call people to withdraw from the things of the world through sacrifice and self-flagellation. Our call is different. God's Spirit, who dwells within, causes us to yearn for that which won't pass away. We look with spiritual eyes and see things as they really are and can't help but be drawn to our living Lord.

People throughout Scripture understood this. Eternity gripped their imaginations, affecting everything they said or did. Three things are clear from their lives: This world was not their home, all that they had was God's and they valued an eternal inheritance. Their lives were a prayer—a Prayer of Detachment. Today we will look at two of these.

This World Is Not My Home

> This world is not my home, I'm just a passing through.
> My treasures are laid up somewhere beyond the blue.
> The angels beckon me from heaven's open door,
> and I can't feel at home in this world anymore.[4]

The words of this old hymn say it all. When we are spiritually reborn, we no longer feel at home in this world. Like Paul, we may be drawn to stay for the sake of the kingdom, but everything in us hungers to be with the Lord.

God's people throughout history obeyed Him against all odds, remaining faithful to the end. Why? "All these died in faith, without receiving the promises, but having seen them and having welcomed them from a distance, and having confessed that they were *strangers and exiles on the earth*" (Hebrews 11:13).

They knew this world was not their home. Abraham left great wealth and social security, wandering as a nomad to fulfill God's plan. Stephen's face shone as he was violently murdered, for he "gazed intently into heaven and saw the glory of God" (Acts 7:55).

Paul affirmed that here he was simply an earthen vessel for an eternal treasure; therefore he could be "afflicted in every way, but not crushed; perplexed, but not despairing; persecuted, but not forsaken; struck down, but not destroyed" (2 Corinthians 4:8–9). He suffered imprisonments, beatings beyond number, shipwrecks, hunger, thirst, exposure to the elements and continual attempts on his life (2 Corinthians 11:23–27). What was his conclusion through all this?

> For momentary, light affliction is producing for us an eternal weight of glory far beyond all comparison, while we look not at the things which are seen, but at the things which are not seen; for the things which are seen are temporal, but the things which are not seen are eternal (2 Corinthians 4:17–18).

For those who suffer in this life, the hope of an eternal home sustains and motivates. But what of those whose life is full of ease, free from the struggle for survival which much of the world endures? What of affluent Christians who are comforted by their possessions and encouraged by their successes? What of people like me?

In loving the world we experience our greatest loneliness, unaware that our heart cries for a city which is to come. We are strangers here, and no matter how comfortable we make our stay, we will always feel the pangs of homesickness.

I have never known hunger or thirst or any real need. Yet I do know the distress of an unsettled soul. I'm aware that comfort comes only when I count everything as loss in light of knowing Christ. But in a world that flaunts its gaudy baubles in my face, I must be reminded that this is not my home. I am a pilgrim on a journey and one day I will reach my eternal destination.

Our life on earth is a breath. The Prayer of Detachment pleads, "Lord, startle me, stir me with this reality." David prayed: "LORD, make me to know my end . . . let me know how transient I am" (Psalm 39:4). As this truth grips our hearts, we see what a waste it is to build kingdoms of comfort in a world that will soon pass away. In faith, we fix our eyes on a city whose architect and builder is God himself—we long to be clothed with our dwelling from heaven (2 Corinthians 5:1–2). This world is not our home.

All That I Have Is His

Several months ago I began to consistently pray a Prayer of Detachment. I knew God wanted to do a deeper work in me in this area. I was taken aback by how He answered.

We suffered a serious financial setback, which put us in debt. Within a few days our finances were in shambles and we were devastated. We had always been careful managers of our money, rarely borrowed, and never depended on credit cards. Beyond that, we gave faithfully to the work of God's kingdom.

My husband and I assessed the situation, looking carefully at our budget, finding ways to cut we had never dreamed possible. There were things we could do that wouldn't solve all our problems, but definitely encouraged us.

The next morning as I came to the Lord in prayer, I heard His gentle voice: "Tricia, you have taken great measures to accomplish your financial goals and get on stable ground. You are willing to sacrifice and do so much. But my heart is grieved. You have never done anything like this for the sake of my kingdom."

I argued with God, "Lord, I'm more faithful in giving than anyone I know. Even when we were struggling seminary students not knowing how we would make it, we always gave You Your part."

As soon as I said those words, my heart was pierced. God's part? Where did I get that idea? How could I have assumed that I had the rights to anything? God never gave me the option of private ownership, no matter how much I gave back to Him. All that I have is His. As this truth settled, I had to repent.

The day the Israelites were to enter the Promised Land, God told them to remember who had brought them there and how He had provided. He warned them that affluence causes people to forget who their source is, thinking they have achieved success on their own. "But you shall remember the LORD your God, for it is He who is giving you power to make wealth, that He may confirm His covenant which He swore to your fathers, as it is this day" (Deuteronomy 8:18).

When I embrace the truth that all that I have is His, I am free from the stranglehold possessions and success can have. I am content no matter what the circumstances, for I know that I brought nothing with me and can take nothing out of this world (1 Timothy 6:7). Like Paul, I "know how to get along with humble means, and I also know how to live in prosperity" (Philippians 4:12).

If all that I have is His, God can do what He wants with it. There is no easier way to become detached from the things of this world than to live out this truth.

Practicing Prayer: Pinning Down His Perspective

Heart Preparation

Becoming Attached: Take some time to thank God for all the ways He has blessed your life, specifically for eternal life and your relationship with Him. Focus your mind and heart on who He is. Read quietly Psalm 34:1–10, personalizing it. Taste for yourself the goodness of God—His complete provision for all your needs. Rest for a few minutes in His presence.

Becoming Detached: Read James 4:1–5 and 1 Timothy 6:7–10. What does this say about the things of the world? Why do you think an attachment to this world is so threatening to our faith?

Read Philippians 4:6,11–13. What secret had Paul learned? How do you think he came to this understanding?

Read Titus 2:11–12. What are we to deny? How are we to live today? To what should we look forward?

Spend some time in prayer meditating on the following question: *Lord, if I truly embraced these principles, how different would my life look?*

This world is not my home:
All that I have is His:

Write a prayer in your journal, asking for help, guidance, and strength to do what God is calling you to do. Pray for a heart of detachment from the world.

DAY TWO: WHAT WILL REALLY LAST?

I Have An Eternal Inheritance

Recently I helped my ninety-one-year-old grandmother, who could no longer live alone, sort through her things. It was a sobering experience. In one day, Grandmother's life was narrowed down to a suitcase and a box.

Ever since, as I look around my own house with personal touches and meaningful memories, I am reminded that there will come a time to pare down until all that's left fits in a suitcase and a box. And even that will not enter eternity.

If our hope is in this life alone, we must despair. But Grandmother's inheritance is not in a suitcase and a box. A glimpse of this appeared in a letter of thanks my father wrote to her many years before. He tells of all the things she taught him and gave him, but most of all he thanks her for one special childhood memory.

It's the memory of being outside our farmhouse in Alabama and hearing you talking inside the house when I knew no one else was with you. I just had to peek in to discover who this was that my mother so earnestly conversed with . . . what a joy it has been to discover that you were simply talking to God our Father—about me, the crops, Dad, all the things mothers are concerned about.

Nothing we build on earth can compare to the treasure that eternity holds. Jesus tells us that our Father has chosen gladly to give us the kingdom and therefore we can invest in unfailing treasures there (Luke 12:32–34). He reminds us that we don't work for food that perishes, but for enduring eternal food upon which He has set His seal (John 6:27).

Moses walked away from a life of ease and wealth, "choosing rather to endure ill-treatment with the people of God . . . considering the reproach of Christ greater riches than the treasures of Egypt; for he was looking to the reward" (Hebrews 11:25–26). Jesus wants us to understand and treasure our eternal reward above anything the world offers. He knows that what we treasure will enslave our hearts (Matthew 6:21). How free we are, when our hearts are enslaved by eternity. Then we can truly detach from all that vies for our allegiance.

The Prayer of Detachment fixes our eyes on eternal life in the presence of the living God. We long for everything we do to point to this, and work diligently for the joy of bringing many others with us. This is the secret to being in the world, but not of it.

Practicing Prayer: Eternity in My Heart

Heart Preparation

Becoming Attached: Consider the things eternity holds for you: intimacy with Jesus Christ, freedom from all pain, endless praise and worship with saints of all ages and nations, to name a few. Reflect on these for a time. Read Revelation 5:1–13. Imagine yourself in the throne room of the King. Look into His face and thank Him for all you have. Worship in words or song.

Becoming Detached: Read Luke 12:14–21. What does Jesus warn concerning greed? How do you think you can guard against the materialism that permeates our culture?

What does Jesus call someone who acts as if their inheritance is in this lifetime? Why?

What would it take for you to be "rich toward God?"

What are you doing right now that will last for eternity?

What won't last?

Prayerfully consider what changes you may need to make to be detached from this world's treasures and invest more freely in eternity. Write a prayer of commitment in your prayer journal.

DAY THREE: WHAT DO I DETACH FROM?

Michael Card, modern-day spiritual balladeer, tells of a recurring vision in which he sees a path disappearing in the distance. Both sides of the path are strewn with various things—a cloak, a cane, an expensive car with the door open and keys in the ignition, etc. All these things people have left behind to follow Jesus. He says that in his vision, he keeps looking for things he has left for the sake of Christ. The simple words of his song conclude: *It's hard to imagine the freedom we find from the things we leave behind.*[5]

Through the Prayer of Detachment, we throw things aside in order to follow the narrow path that leads to eternal life. Every day we shed like a snake in summer the skin that no longer offers the security it once did. In this we find freedom and perhaps begin to understand what it means to carry the yoke of Jesus whose burden is easy and load is light.

How do we know what these things are? It is simple but not necessarily easy. We must leave behind anything that keeps us from being fully Christ's. It could be the dresses in our closets or the cars in our garage, our drive for status or the success we have already achieved. It might be our desperate

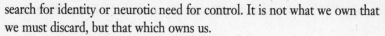

search for identity or neurotic need for control. It is not what we own that we must discard, but that which owns us.

We ask ourselves some hard questions:

What consumes my thoughts and plans?

What holds my dearest allegiance?

Who or what tells me who I am?

What gives me security and comfort?

What makes me feel whole and complete?

Who meets my deepest needs?

In answering these questions, we discover what holds us in its grasp. Most things fall into one of three categories: material possessions, personal success, and interpersonal relationships. Let's look at each one.

Material Possessions

It is not things, but the meaning we give to them that keep us from being completely attached to Christ. When our life consists of what we own, Jesus likens us to fools who will be taken completely by surprise when it all goes up in smoke (Luke 12:15–20). It doesn't matter whether we have a lot or a little, but what value we give it.

Dallas Willard notes that we can be deceived on either side of this coin. While having much may delude us into a false sense of security, having nothing does not necessarily free us. "We do not have to own things to love them, trust them, even serve them. The percentage of those in bondage to wealth is no greater among the rich than among the poor."[6]

What do the things you own mean to you? Do you find identity in them? Do they comfort you? Do they provide a sense of control and well-being? Are you driven by a need for more and more?

Or are you depressed by your lack of things? Do you find yourself thinking if you only had this or that, or a little more than you have, that you would be happy? Or are you so busy accumulating more that you don't have time to even ask why?

In order to crush the idol of materialism, we must have a grasp of how it affects us personally. Does the pull of prosperity persuade us to build bigger and better barns here on earth, while making few eternal investments? Do we trust God or cling to the stock market for daily sustenance? Can we hold our possessions lightly? Are we looking for opportunities to give away more and more?

The Prayer of Detachment asks for an eternal view of temporal things. In it we learn to seek God's kingdom and its righteousness, to store up treasures that cannot be destroyed by market crashes or bombs or earthquakes or floods, and we live with the confidence that everything else will be provided when we do.

Personal Success

In this world our worth hangs in the balance on scales fixed with phony weights. The result is confusion, chaos, and incessant busyness. Thomas Merton describes many of us as "blinded by desire for ceaseless motion, constant sense of achievement, famished with a crude hunger for results, for visible and tangible success. . . ."[7]

It's a crazy world that idolizes athletes, actors, and rock stars. Yet the church has bought the lie. When one of these accepts Christ, we nod in affirmation at the great gift the kingdom of God has been given. Only in contemplation of our Lord can we see the deception.

In God's kingdom the heroes are usually quiet ones. The mom who rejects corporate ladder climbing in favor of building blocks with her babies . . . the elderly woman who prays for her pastor day in and day out on arthritic knees . . . the disabled teenager who serves meals to the homeless every Wednesday. These people are everywhere, but they ask for no glory and seek no status. They have learned the freedom of detachment from worldly success.

My father was this kind of hero. In the prime of his career his boss came to him. "Jim, you are great at your job and everyone likes you, but without more education, you will never go any further than you are right now. Why don't you go back to school at night—your future really depends on it."

He lasted one semester. One day he said to our family, "You know—I can't work all day, go to school at night, spend time with you, and find time to do the Lord's work. I just can't keep doing this."

Dad never advanced again in his job. But every week for twenty years, a new group of students came through the training school where he taught. Each Friday at the end of school, Dad shared his testimony and led in prayer.

When he passed away at sixty-four, Dad's memorial service gave testimony to the choices he had made in life. His former boss called him "the Billy Graham of Southland" (the corporation he worked for). We received letters from people all over the world who had been impacted by him, many in that short week at school. Dad lived with eternity in his heart. He embodied the Prayer of Detachment. Today he enjoys its rewards.

There is nothing wrong with success. But at what cost? What impact are we having on that which will not pass away? What accomplishments have we made that will outlast the next paycheck or performance evaluation?

And what do we believe about what we achieve? Does it represent who we are? Does it tell us how much we are worth? Do we even take the time to ask these kinds of questions?

When we pray for detachment from the drive for personal success, we may be challenged to make radical changes in the way we live our lives. When we look quietly into the face of our Father, we see things very differently and find ourselves longing for another kind of success—one with eternal consequences. As Thomas à Kempis wrote: "Blessed are the ears that catch the pulses of the divine whisper, and give no heed to the whisperings of this world.[8]

Interpersonal Relationships

God made us for each other. From the beginning He said it wasn't good for man to be alone. Through relationships we discover the joy of caring, encouraging, exhorting, even laying down our lives. Relationships are a beautiful part of God's plan for mankind. But something has gone awry.

In this fallen world, we tend to come together not to give, but to get. We cling to each other, longing for an identity that only Christ can give. Such desperate dependency shows up in many ways—in the boss who feels threatened when he can't control every move of his employees, and in the woman who stays in a relationship to be abused day in and day out.

It can be more subtle than that. When we feel afraid upon walking into a room full of people, or run from necessary confrontation, we are entrusting our identity to unknown names and formless faces. When relationships of any kind define us, we are dangerously and compulsively attached. Nothing is less satisfying or more consistently painful.

There is a great deal of teaching, even within the church, about how we need each other. We say things like: *I need you to accept me as I am . . . I need you to validate my feelings . . . I need you to affirm me as a person . . . I need you to admire and respect me . . . I need, I need, I need.* These are all things we should do for each other out of love. But when we require them to prop up our ever-slipping identity, we are attached to others in a way that brings nothing but bondage and defeat.

Jesus set the example for us to follow in interpersonal relationships: He loved those who denied or betrayed him. He confronted and rebuked those who were out of line. He turned to His Father when, as He suffered great agony of soul, His closest friends took a nap. And He asked God to forgive those who were taking His life. He never looked to others to support His identity—and neither should we.

When we experience the Prayer of Detachment, we no longer need the affirmation of others, for we find it in the face of Christ. As one writer puts it: "I love you, I say, but I do not need you to tell me who I am. For the Lord himself does that, when he whispers his love in my ear every day. Every day he creates me anew and sharpens my identity by grace."[9]

Steps to Simplicity

In the simple lifestyle, one seeks to live with wisdom in this world while wholly committed to an eternal perspective. It requires discipline and planning. Here are some ideas to begin:

- *Prayerfully distinguish between needs and wants. Buy what you need, but always seek God's will concerning wants.*
- *For large items (whether needs or wants), refuse to buy on impulse. Take time, seek counsel, pray thoroughly before buying a car, house, boat, etc.*
- *Find a way for you and your family to minister to those less fortunate than you. This brings a balanced perspective into our affluent world.*
- *At least once a year, evaluate how much of your material resources are directly impacting eternity. Commit to making the percentage larger each year.*
- *Eliminate unsecured debts and determine not to use credit again. (This is on anything that depreciates with time—cars, etc.)*
- *Buy that which will last and use it until it wears out, whether it is a car, coat, or bathrobe.*
- *Regardless of how much money you have, continually look for ways to cut costs, freeing up more money for eternal things. Shopping at thrift stores, trading with friends, sharing meals when eating out, are just a few ideas.*

• *Meditate regularly on Scripture concerning worldly values.*

Other Attachments

There are many other things to which we become unwisely attached: food, TV, music, shopping, hobbies, sports, sex, leisure, movies, etc. The list varies and changes throughout our lifetime, and only as we spend time in God's presence can we see the hold these things have on us. There is no way to live a life of detachment without regular, consistent, heartfelt cries for the Lord to rescue us from the depravity we so easily embrace. We must pray every day and throughout each day the Prayer of Detachment.

Practicing Prayer: Attacking Our Attachments

Heart Preparation

Becoming Attached: Welcome the presence of the Holy Spirit within you today. Ask the Spirit to reveal truth to your heart. Read the story of the cross in Luke 23:26–46. Sit quietly and meditate on Jesus as Redeemer. See His beaten body, nail-pierced hands and feet. Think on the price of His precious blood with which He purchased your salvation. Look into His eyes of love. See Him looking at you—doing this for you alone. Receive the love He pours out to you from the cross. Let your heart be drawn into adoration, rest, and quietness.

Becoming Detached: In Scripture we are warned to be careful, to be wise, not to be caught off guard and slowly slip into a carnal love for *things*. One way we can be careful is to evaluate what messages we allow ourselves to receive into our minds and homes. Consider the categories in the list below, and any others, asking yourself probing questions such as:

- How much time in a given day or week do I allow this avenue to feed my mind and heart?
- What are the messages it sends me?
- How does it strengthen my attachment to the world?

1. TV
2. Hobbies/Recreation
3. Work/Career
4. Education
5. Media (newspaper, magazines, etc.)
6. Movies
7. Relationships
8. Clubs/ Community Events

Now, consider each category in light of the truths from Days One and Two. Ask God to show you what place each of these would have in your life if you lived these truths:

- This World is Not My Home
- All That I Have Is His
- I Have an Eternal Inheritance

Offer a simple prayer of commitment to the Lord to seek His will in the coming weeks as you learn to live the Prayer of Detachment.

DAY FOUR: HOW DO I BECOME DETACHED?

Twenty years ago my husband and I flew into a tiny village in the Alaskan bush to begin a Christian work. We were allowed to bring only the bare necessities for life in a small cabin. Getting ready to go was tough. I eliminated, then eliminated some more, and then eliminated even more, finally amazed at how little we really needed in order to get by.

This is similar to the process of detachment. In view of our eternal destiny and short life-span on earth, we ask God to eliminate those things we really don't need. At first it may seem little, but as we grow in Christ, we will see more and more of that which hinders complete attachment to Him.

When these things are taken away, we may be surprised at what they meant to us. Fenelon notes that "we don't feel the hairs on our head until someone pulls one out."[10]

When we pray the Prayer of Detachment, God responds like a surgeon lancing a wound, moving quickly and decisively to rid us of that which has infected our attachment to Him.

By now you are probably aware of at least one thing or area of life from which you long to be detached. You may have begun to pray the Prayer of Detachment. There are three things that will help:

- Pray for a change of heart.
- Put self to death.
- Set your mind on things above.

As we look at each of these, consider the area God has already shown you.

A Change of Heart

No prayer requires such a radical heart shift as the Prayer of Detachment. This goes against everything within us and everything without. Even loved ones or other believers may not understand the decisions that result from our Prayer of Detachment.

Discipline alone does not ensure detachment from the world. We need hearts that see as God sees. He will change how we feel about things if we

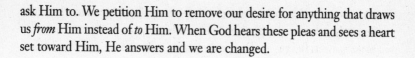

ask Him to. We petition Him to remove our desire for anything that draws us *from* Him instead of *to* Him. When God hears these pleas and sees a heart set toward Him, He answers and we are changed.

Death to Self

This is painful for we are putting to death our own desires, needs, plans, and goals. Yet, we must not give heed to the hurt. We seek in all things to be crucified to the world and the world to us (Galatians 6:14). "In pure love, which is completely detached and abandoned, the soul feeds itself in silence on the cross and on its union with Jesus Christ crucified, without any reversion to its own suffering."[11]

Jesus put it simply: "If any one wishes to come after Me, let him deny himself, and take up his cross and follow Me" (Matthew 16:24). The Prayer of Detachment requires death to self—in practice as well as principle. We do not tame our desires, nor can we discipline our addictions. They must be nailed to the cross, moment by moment, as we cling to the Spirit who indwells us.

Seek Things Above

Daily we are faced with an unprecedented onslaught of information. We are told minute by minute what we should do, think, feel, wear, eat, and enjoy. Our minds are fertile ground for the fools who gain access through TV, radio, newspapers, magazines, etc. There is only one way to keep from being molded by these things: being "transformed by the renewing of your mind" (Romans 12:2). This is what enables us to do the will of God.

Once we have sought to put self to death, we must saturate our minds with all that brings life. Paul categorizes these things for us: whatever is true, honorable, right, pure, lovely, of good repute, excellent, and worthy of praise

(Philippians 4:8). We are to focus on these things day in and day out.

Recently it became apparent that I was losing my ability to enjoy TV and most movies. Because I am trying to set my mind on the things of Christ, I feel uncomfortable with immoral sex and gratuitous violence, no matter how entertaining they may be. What saddens me is how long I have filled my mind with it, dismissing the depravity.

We seek first the kingdom of God, continually setting our minds on things above (Matthew 6:33; Colossians 3:1–3). When we feel the pull of worldly enticements, we turn our heart quickly to the One who overcame the world on our behalf. When we find we've slipped into practices and plans that have nothing to do with eternity, we call out to our Shepherd, who leads us back to paths of righteousness.

Above all, we flood our minds and lives with God's Word. We meditate on it, pray through it, read it, memorize it, and study it whenever we can. We are reprogramming our fallen minds and we must be diligent and purposeful if we are to stand a chance against the evil one who constantly targets our hearts.

When I began to pray the Prayer of Detachment several months ago, I knew material possessions had a great hold on my heart. I memorized Matthew 6:19–33, a passage on priorities and God's provision for me. Every day I said it aloud at least once. Most mornings I meditated on some part of it.

Several phrases from it continue to ring in my mind throughout the day: *Where your treasure is, there will your heart be also . . . no one can serve two masters . . . either he will hate the one and love the other, or he will hold to one and despise the other . . . O [you] of little faith . . . your heavenly Father knows that you need all these things . . . seek first His kingdom and His righteousness.* God is using His word to prepare the soil of my heart for much needed change.

Attachment to Christ

None of these steps will bring lasting change without a passion for Christ. We lose our love for all else only as we find life in relationship with

Him. As we let go of worldly attachments, it is because we no longer need them to provide us with hope, peace, meaning and identity. Jesus gives us all these and more as our hearts are bound more completely to Him.

Practicing Prayer: Diligence in Detachment

Heart Preparation

Becoming Attached: Consider the things Christ left behind to save you. What did it cost Him? Spend some time meditating on these things (see Philippians 2:5–8). Thank God for all He has done, especially as it relates to you personally. Write a prayer of thanksgiving in your prayer journal.

Becoming Detached: Read Matthew 16:24–27. What do each of these things mean to you personally:

Denying yourself:

Taking up your cross:

Following Christ:

How can you lose your life in order to find it? Have you experienced this? Why or why not?

Consider the things from which you long to be detached. Write a plan in your prayer journal (using the steps we've looked at) for how you will find freedom from them:

Prayer for a change of heart

Death to self

Setting your mind on things above

DAY FIVE: SOLITUDE: ALONE, BUT NOT LONELY

Jews have long practiced *hitbodedut*, (aloneness): a time when they separate themselves from the world in order to meditate upon God. "The soul, seeking solitude, seeking quiet, searches out a place where the sounds of the world recede. Once that place is found, the spirit can stand single before its Creator. Free from distraction, the soul finds through the surrounding silence an avenue back to God."[12]

Jesus often experienced *hitbodedut*. Before His earthly ministry began, He spent forty days and nights with only the Father. Throughout His ministry, He left the disciples to be alone—usually early in the morning or throughout the night. The Garden of Gethsemane was familiar long before His final hours. It was His custom to go there for solitude and silence.

If Jesus regularly spent hours alone with His Father, how much more must we? We cannot sense the companionship of Christ in the crowded arena of life, if we haven't learned to languish alone in His presence. We won't recognize His gentle whisper amidst the raucous resonance of our fallen world, unless we know the nuances of His precious voice by heart. These things are learned in solitude with Him.

When we are more at home with the world and its inhabitants than God, we are in desperate need of detachment. We must passionately pursue Jesus, who alone can set us free. "And when He enters in and sups with us and we with Him, what unspeakable joy! At last we are Home. We are on the Rock. Life's end is in God, as its beginning and middle is in God."[13]

Hindrances to Solitude

It is rarely the crises of life that keep us from God. In fact these usually drive us to dependency on Him. Our struggle is with the daily busyness that consumes our life in bite-size pieces. As believers, we may feel safe because we are "working for the kingdom." As long as we maintain some semblance of sanity, we deny our deep need for solitude with God.

Yet we know a gnawing hunger within, a dissatisfaction with things as they are. The Prayer of Detachment cries for insight into what we are feeding our soul. If we stop and evaluate, we will see we are starving for sustenance of another kind. When we begin to feel the emptiness in our gut, we must determine to practice the discipline of solitude. It is not easy, but our survival depends on it.

Fasting and Solitude

Fasting is little understood or discussed in the church today. Yet Scripture is clear that it can and should be a part of our spiritual life.[14]

While others have written extensively on the subject,[15] we will discuss it here only as it relates to the Prayer of Detachment.

Fasting is abstaining from food and/or drink for a specific period of time with a spiritual purpose. Its benefits can include personal purity, power in prayer, spiritual discernment, and a greater experience of God's presence.

Fasting is important as we seek to detach from the world because it causes us to be aware of the hold even our basic physical drives have on us. These are symbolic of all the other things that demand our devotion.

When we fast, we quickly discover how much food means to us—how much pleasure it brings. I can skip meals due to busyness without even noticing, but when I fast, it seems all I can think of is food. I recognize my own neediness and the power my flesh has over me.

Dallas Willard notes the impact fasting can have on detachment: "Since food has the pervasive place it does in our lives, the effects of fasting will be diffused throughout our personality. In the midst of all our needs and wants, we experience the contentment of the child that has been weaned from its mother's breast."[16]

My limited experiences with fasting have taught me how much I need God, how attached I am to things of this world, and how little sacrifice I make in my relationship with Him. When I fret and fuss at the suffering fasting brings my body, I realize how little my life revolves around the living Christ.

The Prayer of Detachment can be greatly helped by a consistent discipline of fasting. I usually practice fasting for a day at a time. Throughout the day I worship, enjoying God's presence as I focus on what Jesus means to me. I also try to get alone with God for a couple of extended prayer times. Some days seem dry and on others I fail miserably by midday. Yet God uses these times to gently wean me from contentment with external things.

I noted before what radical change is required for the Prayer of Detachment. Fasting can be the key to "unlock doors where other keys have failed; a window opening up new horizons in the unseen world; a spiritual weapon of God's providing, 'mighty, to the pulling down of strongholds.' "[17]

❦ ❦

Fasting for Detachment

There are many things from which we can fast that will stimulate growth in the Prayer of Detachment. Some of these are listed below. During your fast, plan to:

- *Meditate on key verses.*
- *Keep a prayer journal of your experience.*
- *Share the experience with someone else.*
- *Evaluate what God's will is concerning the future.*

Meals: Matthew 4:3–4, 5:6, Philippians 3:18–19
(Begin with missing one meal per week. Let this progress into longer fasts.)
Media: Romans 8:6; Philippians 4:8; Isaiah 33:15
(Eliminate outside sources of influence, such as TV, radio, movies, newspapers, etc. for a period. Spend that same amount of time seeking godly teaching.)

Potential Addictions: 1 Corinthians 9:27; 1 Peter 2:11

(These may include chocolate, pastries, fried foods, etc., tobacco, sports, leisure activities. Abstain for a time from whatever tends to be addicting for you.)

Alcohol: Proverbs 20:1; Ephesians 5:18

Unnecessary Talking: Proverbs 13:3; James 3:6

(Commit to listening rather than speaking whenever possible.)

Eating Out: Psalm 41:1, Proverbs 19:17, 23:21

(Save what money you would have spent eating out, even for fast foods, to a meaningful cause, such as feeding the homeless.)

Unnecessary Spending: Isaiah 55:1–2, Luke 8:14

(Buy only what is necessary. Keep a notebook of the things you would have bought without this discipline.)

The Purpose of Solitude

As Thomas Merton notes, solitude is not our goal, but rather a means to an end.[18]

Our goal is to love God and be loved by Him. When we withdraw from all the "vain things that charm us most," and set our eyes on our Beloved, we experience the depths of joy. In this we see the futility of attachment to things that are deteriorating before our eyes and we wonder how they could have had such a hold on our hearts.

Significant things take place in private moments with our Creator. Henri Nouwen encourages us with his poignant words:

> In solitude we can listen to the voice of him who spoke to us before we could speak a word, who healed us before we could make any gesture for help . . . who loved us long before we could give love

to anyone. It is in this solitude that we discover that being is more important than having, and that we are worth more than the result of our efforts.[19]

The Prayer of Detachment is answered in the silence when we see God face-to-face, and the "things of earth grow strangely dim in the light of His glory and grace."

Practicing Prayer: Solitude and Detachment

Heart Preparation

Becoming Attached: Read Psalm 96 out loud. Rewrite the Psalm in your journal, personalizing the words of praise (e.g.: *I will sing unto you, O Lord, a new song . . . all the earth will sing with me; we will sing to you and bless your name, telling everyone everywhere how you saved us.*)

Take some time to focus on the Lord, being aware of the quiet and solitude around you. Commit this time to Him.

Becoming Detached: Read Matthew 4:1–11. How long was Jesus alone? What did He do during this time?

Look at each of the things with which Satan tempted Jesus. What might these be in your life?

What do you think happened during Jesus' time of solitude and fasting that enabled him to resist the pull of worldly attachments?

How much solitude do you practice?

For the next several days, commit to taking at least five minutes a day to be alone to pray the Prayer of Detachment. Consider what messages you have been receiving from the world around you and how they are impacting your decisions. Then, focus on Christ, evaluating these messages in light of all He stands for. Commit to making these times regular and of longer duration as you grow in this area.

Moving Forward

The Prayer of Detachment requires much. It is difficult, and yet clearly what Jesus demonstrated while on earth. I long for the singularity of focus of Jesus, Paul, Peter, and John. They knew why they were here and clung to that in the midst of a world that rejected all they stood for.

I want to know Jesus so intimately that I am not lured for even an instant by the enticements I face daily. While I often look at my progress with discouragement, I remember the time when I was not even aware of my divided loyalties. Being in the battle is the most important thing. Jesus promises to accomplish the rest.

At times the battle takes us into the wilderness, and we aren't sure what God is doing. We sense confusion, face darkness, and perhaps even despair. Such times are an important part of God's plan in our lives. In the next chapter, we will discover the secret of growth through the dark nights of our Christian journey.

Notes

1. Brennan Manning, *The Signature of Jesus on the Pages of Our Lives* (Sisters, Ore.: Multnomah Press, 1992), p. 51.
2. Alexander Whyte, *Lord, Teach Us to Pray* (New York: George H. Doran Company), p. 35.
3. Francois Fenelon, *Christian Perfection* (New York: Harper & Row, 1947), p. 71.
4. Anonymous, Public Domain.
5. Michael Card, *Immanuel, Reflections on the Life of Christ* (Nashville: Thomas Nelson, 1990), p. 119.
6. Dallas Willard, *The Spirit of the Disciplines* (New York: HarperSanFrancisco, 1991), p. 199.
7. Thomas Merton, *New Seeds of Contemplation* (New York: New Direction Books, 1961), p. 158.

8. Thomas à Kempis, *The Imitation of Christ* (New York: Grosset & Dunlap, 1952), p. 119.

9. Emily Griffin, *Clinging, the Experience of Prayer* (San Francisco: Harper and Row, 1984), p. 63.

10. Francois Fenelon, *Christian Perfection* (New York: Harper and Row, 1947), p. 161.

11. Fenelon, p. 88.

12. David J. Wolpe, *In Speech and in Silence: The Jewish Quest for God* (New York: H. Holt, 1992), p. 191.

13. Thomas Kelly, *The Eternal Promise* (New York: Harper & Row, 1966), p. 115.

14. See Matthew 4:1–11; John 4:32–34; Matthew 6:16–18; Luke 12:33; Philippians 3:19; Romans 16:18; Acts 9:9; 1 Corinthians 6:13 and 7:3–5, among many others.

15. See Arthur Wallis, *God's Chosen Fast*, and Bill Bright, *The Coming Revival*.

16. Willard, p. 168.

17. Arthur Wallis, *God's Chosen Fast* (Fort Washington, Penn.: Christian Literature Crusade, 1968), p. 8.

18. Thomas Merton, *Contemplative Prayer* (New York: Herder and Herder, 1969), p.154.

19. Henri Nouwen, *Out of Solitude* (Notre Dame: Ave Maria Press, 1990), p. 22.

SEVEN

PRAYER THROUGH THE DARK NIGHT

Turn your soul, I say, to walk toward God when all seems blackest and there is no light of His presence to be seen anywhere. Though this seems harsh at first, you will soon understand how this journey through dryness and darkness is God's chosen way of purging your soul.

John of the Cross

As a child I loved Jesus. As a teenager I tried to give Him my whole life. It was an idyllic life for the first sixteen years. I lived in one place, grew up with the same friends, attended a small local church and neighborhood school. I was happy. Then we moved 800 miles away. Nothing could have prepared my young sheltered heart for the aching loneliness I faced in that strange new place.

It was my first taste of the dark night of the soul as God ripped everything that once brought security from my life. These words resonate from my teenage diary: *How do I know what I want? What I need? Or what is best for me? I want happiness—where is it found? I want strength—why does it escape me? I want what will give me joy and peace—how long must I wait for it? Oh God, how long?*

Waiting, wandering and weeping . . . these are the landmarks of the dark night. If you are serious about your call to Christ, you will become well acquainted with them. Perhaps you have already.

We wait in darkness because we can do nothing else. We may not feel God's presence, or see His hand in our lives. We wish we could do something, yet God gives no direction.

We wander, feeling completely lost. Our spirits are numb—our passion for God dried up like a withered vine.

We weep because the pain is great and we feel we have no one to turn to. We wonder if even God has abandoned us. Like David we cry out: "My tears have been my food day and night, while they say to me all day long, 'Where is your God?'" (Psalm 42:3).

The term "dark night of the soul" was coined by one who knew the darkness well. John of the Cross, a passionate Christian in sixteenth-century Spain, encountered horrible suffering as a result of his faith. Kidnapped, beaten, and crippled for life, he continued to seek the face of God. Darkness was all he felt; silence all he heard. Then one night after having been imprisoned in a broom closet for six months, God broke through with a message for the world to hear.

John spent the rest of His life teaching about the purpose of the dark night in the life of every believer. His life reflected the light of God's love and peace in the midst of despair. Toward the end of his days, he wrote of hearing God ask, "What reward do you wish for? What reward for all you have done for Me?" John responded, "Nothing else, O Lord, except to suffer for Thee, and for Thy sake to be despised and condemned!"[1]

Though martyred for his faith, John of the Cross's many writings continue to impact our world.

Prayer through the dark night is our source of strength, and hope for transformation. Maybe you have experienced your own darkness, but didn't realize what God was doing. If so, this chapter will be an encouragement. Perhaps you are struggling even now to hold on. There is a purpose in this.

We need not fear the darkness, once we have embraced Prayer Through the Dark Night.

DAY ONE: CHARACTERISTICS OF THE DARK NIGHT

Words about the dark night of the soul may seem depressing. Why should we consider it? Aren't we supposed to be full of joy? Doesn't God have a wonderful plan for our lives? Why should we focus on the negative?

A glance at the dark night may indeed discourage us. Yet, if we take the time to gaze at it from God's perspective, all the parts of our life take on new meaning. Every day—whether it be full of joy or sorrow, dryness, or abundance—is part of God's redeeming work within. Knowing His plan not only steadies us through the toughest moments of faith, but enables us to actually embrace the darkness. We can become like the apostles who rejoiced "that they had been considered worthy to suffer" (Acts 5:41).

The dark night is more than difficult circumstances, yet they play a part. It is more than dryness, yet aridity accompanies it. It is more than sorrow, yet pain may be prevalent. It is no accident, but a gift from our Sovereign Lord to accomplish His purposes in our life.

The dark night is a season when God strips us of things that keep us from going further in our walk with Him. "When we have hit bottom and are emptied of all we thought important to us, then we truly pray. . . . In the midst of the emptying we know that God hasn't deserted us. He has merely removed the obstacles keeping us from a deeper union with Him."[2]

Deserts, darkness, and death characterize the dark night. Perhaps you've known all three. Somehow, God uses dryness in the desert, confusion in the darkness, and despair in the deaths of the dark night to accomplish His lasting work.

Deserts

Do you sometimes wonder if you are going backward in your Christian walk? Do you remember times when God seemed so much more real, when your love for Him was full of life and purpose? Outwardly you trudge on, but deep within you are haunted by questions: Where is God? What is wrong with me? Why can't I find a way out of this? Will I ever know the sweet touch of God's love again?

We can't seem to reclaim what we once had as we wander through the wilderness of faith. God's Word loses its flavor and His people bring little joy to our hearts. We may even question our salvation. We look at others whose lives seem so bright, and wonder where we failed. We don't know what to do, so we wander around, wishing something would change.

❧ ❧

The Marks of a Dark Night

The Mark	*God's Word*	*The Characteristic*
Desert		Dryness

"O God, Thou art my God; I shall seek Thee earnestly; my soul thirsts for Thee, my flesh yearns for Thee, in a dry and weary land where there is no water" (Psalm 63:1).

Darkness		Confusion

"Who is among you that fears the LORD, that obeys the voice of His servant, hat walks in darkness and has no light? Let him trust in the name of the LORD and rely on his God" (Isaiah 50:10).

Death		Despair

"My God, my God, why hast Thou forsaken me? Far from my deliverance are the words of my groaning. O my God, I cry by day, but Thou dost not answer; and by night, but I have no rest. Yet Thou art holy, O Thou who art enthroned upon the praises of Israel" (Psalm 22:1–2).

The desert is a barren place. The streams of living water seem to have dried up. God is present, but the experience of His presence escapes us. Often this comes after we have known great wonders of His grace. Like Elijah after incredible victories in the battle of the gods at Mount Carmel, we find ourselves in the wilderness, questioning the purpose of our life (1 Kings 18–19).

A beautiful young French woman named Jeanne Guyon (see Chapter 2) experienced immense suffering throughout her life. God's sweet hand sustained her through the death of her husband and children, horrible personal disfigurement from smallpox, and severe persecution for her faith. His love filled her every pore and she remained a glorious testimony of faith in the midst of pain.

Then she entered a long, dry spiritual desert. She writes that the emptiness and impotency she faced were worse than any trials she had known before. From prison she agonized: " 'Is it possible,' I cried, 'that I have received so many graces and favors from God only to lose them—that I have loved Him with so much ardor, but to be eternally deprived of Him . . . that my heart has been emptied of all . . . and filled with His blessed presence and love, in order now to be wholly void of divine power and only filled with wanderings. . . ?' "[3]

Darkness

If the characteristic of the desert is dryness, the characteristic of the darkness is confusion. We wait, but nothing happens. We ask, but answers don't come. We may have enough faith to believe God still reigns, but our heart cannot respond to Him. We aren't sure what He wants from us or where to go to find out.

Darkness can be debilitating, even paralyzing. We cannot see one step in front of us, so we freeze. Our lives may be in chaos, yet we are at a loss as to what we can do to change things.

Worst of all, we can't see God or feel His touch. We cry out like David: "Why dost Thou stand afar off, O LORD? Why dost Thou hide Thyself in times of trouble? . . . My heart throbs, my strength fails me; and the light of my eyes, even that has gone from me" (Psalm 10:1; 38:10).

Several years ago I experienced this. My husband and I prayed for a second child for six years, but our pleas seemed to be lost in a dark abyss. This wasn't the first time God had said *no* or *wait* to me, but this seemed different. With each new day my personal pain grew more unbearable. By the sixth year, darkness was my unwelcome companion.

Morning after morning, I sat with my Bible in hand—reading words that lacked meaning, feeling absolutely nothing. There was no action I could take, no truth I could learn. I prayed by faith but my heart felt cold and empty. I just didn't know what to do. All I could do was wait. My feelings of resignation frightened me. Darkness. Silence.

Death

Sometimes the darkness is so great or lasts so long that we begin to despair. Jeremiah cried, "Look and see if there is any pain like my pain . . . [God] has made me desolate, faint all day long" (Lamentations 1:12–13). Job cursed the day he was born: "May that day be darkness . . . for my groaning comes at the sight of my food, and my cries pour out like water" (Job 3:4, 24). David pleaded with God, "How long, O LORD? Wilt Thou forget me forever? . . . How long shall I take counsel in my soul, having sorrow in my heart all the day?" (Psalm 13:1–2).

We suffer depression, anxiety, or overwhelming anger. We want to run, but there is nowhere to go. Confronted with our own frailty, we rail at God. We wonder why we are here, and question if we have the strength to go on living. Nothing comforts us, no thought encourages us.

Our sleep is haunted, our waking hours grim. We believe God has inflicted on us fierce sorrow and then left us alone to deal with it. Worst of all, it feels as if it will never end—this is now our lot in life. In private moments, we may wish we could die.

Prayer Through the Dark Night is unlike any other kind. It means holding on in silence, clinging in darkness, resting in the midst of upheaval. If we learn how to endure, to press through, one day the light will dawn with such force that we'll think we've been blind until now. Tried by fire, our faith can no longer be easily shaken.

Practicing Prayer: Deserts, Darkness, and Death

Heart Preparation

Spend some time quieting your heart before God. Thank Him for His continual presence and purpose in your life. Read Psalm 138 out loud, slowly. Then read it again, changing the words to personalize it. Invite the Holy Spirit to speak, opening your heart to all He may say. Offer this time to God to do as He wills.

Think about your life in Christ. Have there been times when

- you were bored, dry, lacking life or vision?
- you were confused, wondering if God had abandoned you?
- you wanted to give up completely?
- you felt a sense of desperation and nothing seemed to help?

How have you changed as a result of these times?
Do you think God has accomplished His will through them?
Are you in a dark night right now?
Would you describe it as a desert, darkness, or death (or all three)?

As you read the following verses, describe the circumstances and responses of those who have encountered the dark night.

Deserts—The Israelites: Exodus 13:1–5; 16:1–4; 17:1–7

What did the Israelites expect their future to hold?
How did they respond when things weren't as they hoped?
How long were they in the wilderness?
What were God's plan and purpose? (See Deuteronomy 8:2.)

Darkness—Joseph: Genesis 37:5–9, 18–28; 50:15–21

What did Joseph think his life was going to be like?
What was it really like?
What was Joseph able to say about the years of suffering he encountered? (vv. 19–21).

Death—Job: Job 1–2; 42:1–6

Did Job do something to deserve the pain he encountered?
What was the outcome of the years of despair he faced in the death of all he loved? (See 42:5–6.)

Spend some time offering the parts of your life to the Lord. Ask Him for strength to face the darkness and wisdom to embrace His purposes in them. Write a commitment in your prayer journal concerning your future dark nights of faith.

DAY TWO: THE CALL OF THE DARK NIGHT

Can it be that the prophets and priests of twentieth-century Christianity have sold us a bill of goods? Bumper sticker theology abounds: Something *good* is going to happen to you! Expect a miracle! God wants you rich! God wants you happy! God wants you well! Have we diminished the cosmic Christ to a bountiful benefactor?

If so, what do we do with the acute distress, the crashing course of pain that often confronts us? How do we reconcile this god of only good gifts with struggle, suffering, or even sovereign silence? Where can we turn when darkness descends?

Perhaps we have lost something valuable in our attempts to make God knowable, His ways comprehensible to our finite minds. Making God in *our own image* is a dangerous thing. It blinds our eyes and deafens our ears. All we can do is settle for counterfeits of cheap grace and milk-toast mercy.

But there stands Jesus—destitute, beaten, broken, abused, and forsaken. His lonely voice echoes even now: *If anyone wishes to come after Me, let him deny himself, and take up his cross, and follow me* (Matthew 16:24). I can almost see Peter reminiscing over those words . . . remembering the cross . . . reminding us . . . "For you have been called for this purpose, since Christ also suffered for you, leaving you an example for you to follow in His steps" (1 Peter 2:21).

Is it possible that God not only approves, but inflicts the dark night of the soul upon us? If so, why? What infinite purpose might cause Him to do such a thing? Paul reminds us that during those times when we are incapable of even putting words to our prayers, God is causing all things to work together for our good. How? "For whom He foreknew, He also predestined to become conformed to the image of His Son . . . (Romans 8:29)."

God longs for us to look like Jesus from the fiber of our being. To this end, He calls us into the dark night. There, emptied of human goodness and vain spirituality, we can be filled. Into our impoverishment, God pours His pure life and changes us into the image of His precious Son.

The call of the dark night is the unexpected answer to so many of our pleas: "We have asked God for the gift of prayer and he visits us with adversity to bring us to our knees. We have prayed for humility and God levels us with humiliation. We cry out for an increase of faith and God strips us of the reassurances that we had identified with faith."[4]

The call of the dark night is to a deeper place of faith. External supports are removed and internal comforts extinguished. For each of us our dark nights will differ, but the call is the same: *Take up your cross and follow Me.*

Removal of Outer Supports

Our early dark nights may consist of suffering from unpleasant or painful circumstances. Loss is all too familiar: of job, health, reputation, loved ones, desires, dreams, possessions, or personal security. The removal of precious comforts suspends our walk with Christ over an abyss of pain and confusion.

Is this really necessary? Can't we just give our lives to Christ? Won't spiritual disciplines like prayer, Bible study, ministry, or worship produce maturity? Aren't these enough? Not really.

Fenelon likens us to a man who falls into a chasm and will not let go until his hands lose their grip on all the supports at its edge. "The infinite jealousy of God pushes us to this extent, and our self-love makes it a necessity, because we only lose ourselves completely in God when all else fails."[5]

While the false doctrines of peace and prosperity induce guilt for those who suffer, God speaks gently into our pain: "My son, do not regard lightly the discipline of the LORD, nor faint when you are reproved by Him; for those whom the LORD loves He disciplines, and He scourges every son whom He receives" (Hebrews 12:5–6).

My second dark night came in college through a broken engagement. Alone, hurting and desperate for some comfort or escape, I cried out to God. After a few days His voice broke through. *Let go* reverberated in my ears. I wrote those two words on construction paper and taped them to my dorm room ceiling. Through the stripping of my dearest relationship, I learned to cling to the love of Christ. I'm convinced it could have happened no other way at that point in my life. God gave the gift of darkness that I might walk in a more purifying light.

Madame Guyon pleads with us, "Oh poor creatures, who pass your time in feeding upon the gifts of God, and think therein to be the most favored and happy. How I pity you if you stop here, short of the true rest, and cease to go forward to God himself, through the loss of those cherished gifts that you now delight in. . . ."[6]

Do we truly love God? We are most discerning about this when His gifts are torn from our life and we turn to Him in the totality of our desolation.

Removal of Internal Supports

As babes in Christ, we cling to the milk of God's sweet presence. We know such simple joy that following Him is second nature. His love fills us with a comfort we couldn't have imagined we could have for ourselves. It's a wonderful time—this honeymoon of Christian faith.

But the hard work comes in making the marriage work. We don't feel so wonderful anymore. In fact, we may feel absolutely nothing. The first time this happens, we are frightened. Have I lost my faith? Was it all a joke? Is something wrong with me? Where is my joy?

The sweetness of communion with Christ escapes us. Spiritual thirst diminishes, hunger wanes. If we aren't diligent, we will fall away, drawn from worship to worldliness. In the dryness of the dark nights, God is once again stripping us, but this time the surgeon's knife probes deeper. He is cutting away our attachment to our feelings, our need for tangible assurance.

Richard Foster suggests that through this process we develop a "holy distrust for superficial drives and human strivings."[7]

We don't realize how much we need to feel good about our faith, until spiritual desolation encompasses us. We want to throw in the towel.

Not only is there a loss of feelings, but logic escapes us. We cannot imagine why God is doing things this way. Nothing makes sense. We may try to rationalize the path our life has taken, but often this is impossible.

God's holy fire consumes our compulsion to explain the mysteries of our walk with Him. He speaks: " 'My thoughts are not your thoughts, neither are your ways My ways. . . . For as the heavens are higher than the earth, so are My ways higher than your ways, and My thoughts than your thoughts' " (Isaiah 55:8–9).

As young missionaries in Alaska, my husband and I struggled to learn this lesson. The ministry was hard, the fruit of our labor rare. After a year of pouring out our lives, we had only six other Christians in our village of one hundred Eskimos. One night in a drunken stupor, a fifteen-year-old boy murdered two of these beloved believers.

We spent hours crying together, trying to make sense out of this. There was none. We had no answers to the brutal killing of our precious friends. No one did. At some point we simply laid our broken hearts at the foot of the cross. Today, twenty years later, it makes no more sense than it did then. But through that dark night, we were called to release our need to understand, our grasp at human sovereignty. He alone is God—there is no other. In this we rest.

The dark night inevitably calls us to the place where it seems God has abandoned us. We have no sense of His presence, no internal assurance that He walks with us. We feel the door slamming on our prayers. We can't understand why God is so distant when we are trying to be so faithful. The worst part is that nothing we do seems to make a difference. We go to this conference, read this new book, attend this exciting church, and yet the emptiness remains.

Nothing works because God deems it so. One day He will surprise us with a fresh touch, but for now He asks only one thing: "Abide in Me, and I in you" (John 15:4). By faith, we discard all that once connected us to Christ and cling to Him alone. We affirm His presence, though we do not feel Him. Our ears are fine tuned to the least sound He might make, though He doesn't speak.

Darkness is our home. Yet, unlike our Savior who knew the agony of real abandonment by the Father, we are never left alone. "God withdraws every remnant of sweetness so that the soul, in dry faith alone, may cling to the feet of Him whom it knows to be hanging before it on the cross, though in the thick darkness it does not and cannot see Him."[8]

This then is the call of the dark night—to abandon all and follow Jesus Christ to Calvary. Like Him, we persevere, knowing that "for the joy set before us," we can endure the cross. Resurrection hope sustains us as we learn the Prayer Through the Dark Night.

Practicing Prayer: Discovering God's Plan

Heart Preparation

Read Psalm 22:1–2. In prayer, share with God the times (perhaps even now) you have felt as David did. Spend some time in communion with Him, affirming in faith that He hears your cries.

After a time of healing ministry with God, read Psalm 22:3–5, 22–24. By faith, speak the truths found in these verses. (e.g.: Lord, you are holy— set apart from my human way of thinking. You rule from your throne on high, etc.)

Offer yourself to the Lord for this time of meditation.

Read John 12:24 and James 5:7–8. What does this say to you?

What things might God be putting to death in your own dark nights?

What do you think the "precious produce" could be?

See 1 Peter 4:12–19. What admonition are we given in verse 12? verse 13? verse 19?

How would these three things change the way you might view the dark nights you have had or will have in your Christian walk?

Evaluate in prayer the wrong attitudes you may have had toward your own dark nights. Offer them to the Lord. If you have sinned, confess it and receive His cleansing. If you have been weak, rest in His strength. Personalize and write 1 Peter 4:19 in your prayer journal. Say it aloud at least three times as a prayer to God and affirmation for yourself.

DAY THREE: QUESTIONS IN THE DARK NIGHT

The dark night is filled with burning questions: Why me? What have I done to deserve this? Is God mad at me? Have I sinned? Endless soul searching fails to reveal answers to these basic queries.

This is exacerbated by the popular gospel of "health, wealth, and prosperity." If we are sick, we must have sinned. If we suffer financial setbacks, we must not have given enough. If we fail, we must not have had enough faith. Solutions such as these are not only heretical, but they offer no encouragement to those who seek to make Christ their Lord.

We may turn outward to explain the course our lives have taken. We blame our pastor or other spiritual leaders for not feeding us. We think our church has lost its vision. We may even wander from church to church, looking for some relief. It won't come.

Sin, disobedience, apathy, or rebellion in the Christian life do not cause the dark night of the soul (although difficult consequences will result from these). The dark night is not the result of a lifeless church or inadequate spiritual leadership. As dark as these things seem, they differ from the kind of darkness in which our heart, pure and holy before the Lord, cries out to a Presence we no longer sense.

How can we explain this dryness that has no apparent cause? What can we do amidst the thundering storms that threaten to drown our passion for Christ? When we agonize before the Lord and find no answers, what should we conclude about the darkness that now surrounds us? Why is this happening?

The dark night of the soul visits those who love God and relentlessly pursue His will for their lives. It may descend when we pray for greater faith or long for deeper substance to the words we speak. It can come because our loving Father desires to enter a new dimension in relationship with us. It is not the consequence of bad decisions or sinful actions, but rather the flame of God's burning love, branding our hearts more fully with His Name.

Maturity in Christ demands a dance with the dark night. Jesus explained that unless a grain of wheat is buried in the ground and dies, it cannot bear fruit (John 12:24). The dark night is that time in the murky bowels of the earth. As our old self is put to death, fresh seeds of faith take root and begin to spread through the parts of our life.

Brennan Manning calls this a mandatory *crucifixion of the ego*. "That is why mature Christian prayer inevitably leads to the purification of the dark night . . . which buries egoism and leads us out of ourselves to experience God. . . . The sign of the cross is written large on the interior life of every authentic disciple."[9]

So, then, how can we recognize the dark night for ourselves? First, we must be confident before God that our hearts are fully committed to Him. This does not mean that we have no weakness or failure, but our deepest longing is to know Him and make Him Lord. When we feel certain of this, we ask ourselves some questions:

- Has the sweetness of my walk with Christ waned or disappeared?
- Does it seem like I'm going backward instead of forward in my spiritual life?
- Is my commitment to serve God strong, while my feelings don't support it?

- Are things happening that don't make sense in my life?
- Do the normal disciplines of prayer, Bible study, etc., seem to make little difference in how I feel?
- Does prayer seem fruitless, Bible study dry or meaningless, and fellowship with other believers disappointing?
- Do I find myself caught up in busyness, resisting quiet moments with Christ?
- Does the sense of God's presence elude my greatest efforts at communion with Him, though within I know He is there?

If we can answer yes to some or all of these questions, we most likely are experiencing some form of a dark night of the soul. Knowing this changes everything. Instead of fretting and fussing—hoping it will end, embrace it in faith. James encourages, "As an example, brethren, of suffering and patience, take the prophets who spoke in the name of the Lord. Behold, we count those blessed who endured. You have heard of the endurance of Job and have seen the outcome of the Lord's dealings, that the Lord is full of compassion and is merciful" (James 5:10–11).

In the compassion of our Lord, we take comfort. From His example, we take courage. In His promise to never leave or forsake us, we find solace for our souls. And our faith is fortified as we learn to focus on eternal purposes.

Practicing Prayer: Answering the Call

Heart Preparation

Take some time to acclimate your heart before the Lord. Read Isaiah 53:1–6 slowly, personalizing the verses. Thank God specifically for each thing these verses tell you about Him. Write in your prayer journal a response to this kind of love. Ask God to teach you from His heart today.

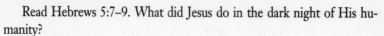

Read Hebrews 5:7–9. What did Jesus do in the dark night of His humanity?

What did He learn from His suffering?

What was the result (v. 9)?

Read Hebrews 12:1.

Consider the areas of your life. In what would you desire greater obedience? What things may be weighing you down, keeping you from running the race with intensity?

Are you willing for God to do whatever it takes to change you in these areas? Even to enter another dark night if need be?

If you struggle to say yes, offer your fears and reservations to Him, asking Jesus to change your heart.

If you are willing, write the following prayer in your prayer journal, and commit to speaking it at least once a day to God.

Lord Jesus, please do all that you must to me,
so that you can do all that you want in and through me.

DAY FOUR: CONDITIONS FOR GROWTH

In her famous allegory *Hinds Feet on High Places*, Hannah Hurnard unveils the heart of the dark night of the soul in a graphic and compelling way. The main character, "Much-Afraid," is on a journey to the high places where she will run like a deer and know perfect rest with the Shepherd at her side. Her companions on the journey are "Sorrow" and "Suffering" and there are many ups, downs, and detours to the high places.

Finally, the sun shines and it seems she will reach her destination. To her dismay, the next turn plunges her down a mountain to a desolate valley. This devastates Much-Afraid and for a moment she considers giving up. She reasons that she does not have to keep following the Shepherd—the choice surely is her own. The terror of that thought engulfs her:

> During that awful moment or two it seemed to Much-Afraid that she was actually looking into an abyss of horror, into an existence in which there was no Shepherd to follow or to trust or to love—no Shepherd at all, nothing but her own horrible self. Ever after, it seemed that she had looked straight down into Hell. At the end of that moment Much-Afraid shrieked—there is no other word for it.
>
> "Shepherd," she shrieked. "Shepherd! Shepherd! Help me! Where are you? Don't leave me!" The next instant she was clinging to him, trembling from head to foot and sobbing over and over again, "You may do anything, Shepherd. You may ask anything—only don't let me turn back. . . . If you can deceive me, my Lord . . . you may, indeed, you may; only don't let me leave you. Don't let anything turn me back. . . ."[10]

This is the cry of the dark night: "Do anything, Lord—anything at all, but don't let me turn back." Everything in us may long to run, to escape to easier places. From the deepest part of our soul, we utter a broken plea: "Don't let me leave You, Lord. . . . Don't let me leave You."

But how do we go beyond mere survival through the dark night? What must we do for God to accomplish His purposes in it? How can we be sure we don't waste our dark nights in the scheme of eternity? What will enable us to do more than just get to the other side? We must still our souls, strive to enter God's rest, and seek God for himself alone.

Stilling Our Souls

There is a quietness that comforts in the core of the dark night. It descends when we let go of our need to understand. David said, "O LORD, my heart is not proud, or my eyes haughty; nor do I involve myself in great matters, or in things too difficult for me. Surely I have composed and quieted my soul; like a weaned child rests against his mother, my soul is like a weaned child within me" (Psalm 131:1–2).

As we choose to let go of our need to explain the events of our life, we learn to be still, to rest against the breast of our Savior—His beating heart soothing, calming us like a child in its father's lap.

During the dark night, we must do this daily. With our mouth, we confess our weakness and confusion, and in the confessing, we let go. Then we choose to be still, trusting by faith in the Presence we may not feel.

This could mean walking away from activity—even "spiritual" activity—until we know how to do only what God calls us to do. The busyness of life, especially the life of faith, can be a great hindrance to a composed and quiet soul. To be still, we must cease activity and motion.

Through the dark night, we sometimes feel little longing to be alone with Christ. The time seems fruitless, the pain unsettling. Yet, if God chooses to speak into our desolation, we will not hear him unless we have quieted all the other sounds.

This is how God moved during the difficult years of my infertility. Day by day I made myself come before Him. I read His Word, though it held little meaning. I wrote in my prayer journal, though it was empty and dry. I voiced my agony, though my hope for a response was negligible. I kept coming, trying to be still in the presence of a God I couldn't find.

One day as I blithely filled in the blanks of a Bible study, from somewhere deep within me, a voice spoke. It was a familiar voice, but one I hadn't heard in so long. His words were clear: "Tricia, your pain is not being caused by your failure to have another child. Your pain is caused by what you have come to believe about me—that I am not fair, that I don't really love you, that I don't have your best interests at heart."

I began to weep in God's presence, confessing that what He said was right. I worshiped Him for His faithfulness, love, mercy, and omnipotence—all that I knew was true about Him. Six years of pain were alleviated in that moment when God chose to reveal himself in a new way. In that moment the dark night was lifted.

I believe I heard God's voice because I had trained myself to be still before Him. In that final year I grappled with God, not hearing anything, not understanding why, not feeling His comfort. But when in His sovereign plan He chose to speak, I was humbled and grateful that I had never stopped listening.

Strive to Enter God's Rest

The Bible is full of paradoxes. We die to live, we give up to gain, we humble ourselves to be lifted up, and we strive to find rest. But the striving through the dark night is not fierce determination or sheer grit based on the strength of our humanness. It is not a series of activities to make us more worthy of God's intervention, nor is it mental gymnastics with positive thoughts until better things come.

God calls us to a rest from our own works, our own achievements, and our own drive to succeed. He calls us to complete, unadorned abandonment to Him. One thing can keep us from this in the midst of the dark night—unbelief (Hebrews 3:19). The Israelites quit believing God when the desert dragged on forty years, and in the end many never experienced the rest God promised.

Don't Build Your Own Fire

Behold, all you who kindle a fire, who encircle yourselves with firebrands, walk in the light of your fire and among the brands you have set ablaze. This you will have from My hand; and you will lie down in torment.

Isaiah 50:11

One of the easiest snares of the dark night is to try to build your own fire. God warns us that this will result in great personal torment. He has placed us in the darkness for a purpose and will remove it when He has accomplished His purposes. Four things can keep us from building our own fire:

- *Reach out to the Father—listen more/ talk and do less.*
- *Release your need to understand, daily.*
- *Reject self-sufficient efforts to change things.*
- *Acknowledge your spiritual poverty moment by moment.*

The writer of Hebrews encourages us to *strive*, to be diligent about following God, even through the darkest deserts of life. We strive to keep from drifting into disobedience. We strive to keep our hearts from being hardened. We strive to hold our faith intact. We strive to be still and know that He is God (Psalm 46:10).

Diligence in prayer develops our muscles of faith through the dark night. Sometimes we may be incapable of crying anything but "Lord, have mercy on me." We question God, jabbing at Him with our lonely fears. This too is prayer, and so much better than indifference or resignation. God absorbs our complaints and holds out His arms to our sin-saturated souls. Yet, when we've finished with our lament, we say as Job did: "Yet I will praise Him." This we must strive to do.

Seek God for Himself

Our duty in the dark night is not complicated. God calls to us: "Who is among you that fears the LORD, that obeys the voice of His servant, that walks in darkness and has no light? Let him trust in the name of the LORD and rely on his God" (Isaiah 50:10).

All that we must learn or do is summed up in one thing: trust and reliance on God. Nothing else matters. When we do not feel the sweet touch of God's grace, we trust Him anyway. When the joyous heights of worship wane, we worship Him anyway. When ministry bears no fruit and fellowship brings disappointment, we serve Him anyway.

When we are weak, spiritually destitute, at the end of our rope, we rely on Him. When we can't find the strength to take another step, we rest in Him. When everything in us wants to hide, we run to Him. We may not feel like it, we may not want to, but we do. We just do.

We live by the mandate that "faith is the assurance of things hoped for, the conviction of things not seen" (Hebrews 11:1). We hope when it seems hopeless. We cling to Him when we want to let go. We follow when we can't see the path ahead. We wait when we've already waited an eternity. When we do, God is pleased (Hebrews 11:2).

We welcome the darkness as a gift—one that enables us to understand the treasure of our living Savior's love. This tiny taste of life without Him compels us to hold Him closer, to let go of everything that keeps us from him. Little "Much-Afraid" learned this lesson in the valley of loss.

The awful glimpse down into the abyss of an existence without Him had so staggered and appalled her heart that she felt she could never be quite the same again. However, it had opened her eyes to the fact that right down in the depths of her own heart she really had but one passionate desire, not for the things that the Shepherd had promised, but for himself. All she wanted was to be allowed to follow him forever.

"Nothing else really matters," she said to herself, "only to love him and to do what he tells me. I don't know quite why it should be so, but it is. All the time it is suffering to love and sorrow to love, but it is lovely to love him in spite of this, and if I should cease to do so, I should cease to exist."[11]

When we come to the place where we say by faith, "I love You, Lord—nothing else really matters," we have learned the dark night's greatest lesson. In seeking God for himself alone, we release our demand for the sense of His presence, the sweetness of His love or the benefits of His benevolence. He is enough—not what He might do or how He might make us feel or what He might give us—He alone is enough.

Practicing Prayer: Letting God Change You

Heart Preparation

Spend a few minutes becoming still before the Lord. Breathe quietly and deeply as you pray the words of David: "O LORD, my heart is not proud, or my eyes haughty; nor do I involve myself in great matters or in things too difficult for me. Surely I have composed and quieted my soul." Repeat this prayer as many times as necessary to experience inner quietness.

Ask God to reveal truth today. Pray for a heart that is open to anything He wants to show you. Offer Him yourself as a living sacrifice.

Read Exodus 33:14 and Matthew 11:29. What are we promised? What do you think this rest is? Have you ever experienced it?

Read Hebrews 4:9–11. In order to experience God's rest, what must we cease from?

Why is this so hard to do during the dark night?

What kinds of things do you find yourself doing when God seems distant or your faith seems dry?

Consider the dark night you are in right now, or one you will encounter in the future. What steps can you take to make sure you:

- Still Your Soul
- Strive to Enter God's Rest
- Seek God for Himself

Write a prayer of commitment concerning these three things in your prayer journal.

DAY FIVE: CHANGES FROM THE DARK NIGHT

The dark night of the soul can change us like no other experience of faith. For every crucifixion, a resurrection awaits and in this we rejoice. The dark night is not some form of penance for failure or punishment for our depravity. God blesses us with the dark night that He might accomplish amazing things. When we embrace this gift of darkness, trusting in Him alone, we will be changed.

Greater Knowledge of Self

God humbles us through the dark night. We begin to see how empty our efforts at change are—how impotent we are to make any difference at all. For in the dark night, there is nothing we can do. When we try, we fail, feeling more helpless than before.

Sometimes we sense such overwhelming sorrow over our inadequacy that we fall on our faces in despair. Like Paul, we cry out, "Wretched man that I am. Who will set me free from the body of this death?" (Romans 7:24). This is the humiliation of the dark night.

Yet God is never more near than when our hearts awaken in horror to their own degradation. He promises, "I dwell on a high and holy place, and also with the contrite and lowly of spirit in order to revive the spirit of the lowly and to revive the heart of the contrite" (Isaiah 57:15).

John of the Cross notes that this humiliation will result in changed attitudes and behavior. As we see ourselves parched and miserable, we cannot consider ourselves better than others. We begin to love and esteem them instead of judging them. We are more willing to be taught—our hearts to submit to instruction.[12]

We come to understand that in our flesh dwells no good thing—our best efforts still miss the mark.

Greater Knowledge of God

Oswald Chambers shares that God trusts us with darkness when He is teaching us something valuable. "His silence is the sign that He is bringing you into a marvelous understanding of himself."[13]

Job said that before his great dark night, he talked about God, but didn't really understand Him. After all the pain he faced, he asks God to teach Him more, saying: "I have heard of Thee by the hearing of the ear; but now my eye sees Thee" (Job 42:5).

The dark night can make the difference between knowing about God and truly knowing Him. When all the accoutrements of faith are removed and we are left with the living God alone, we begin to see Him as He really is. We can never be the same when we do.

A Purer Faith

Christian saints from past centuries talked of the "purgation of the senses," which takes place in the dark night. This means simply that we come to the point where we rely less and less on how we feel about God, and more and more on what He says is true. Our relationship with Him is not founded on experiences of sweetness and joy, but rooted in His unconditional love, which He never ceases to pour out on us.

We obey because we love Him, not because He will be pleased or will reward us with ecstatic experiences. While these things may come, they are no longer the driving force in our faith. Love and love alone compels us. Jesus said, "If you love me, you will keep my commandments." Through the dark night, we come closer to living out the truth of these words.

A Gentle and Peaceful Spirit

Perhaps the most visible change from the dark night is the gentleness and peace that takes root deep within. We are not shaken so easily by external or internal forces that war against our souls. In the darkness we learn to embrace the Sovereignty of Almighty God.

This sense of peace is seen throughout Scripture.

Job said in the midst of his darkest days, "Though He slay me, I will hope in Him" (Job 13:15). David declared after being seized by the Philistines, "This I know, that God is for me. . . . What can man do to me?" (Psalm 56:9–11). Paul, who knew such terrible rejection from within the church and unending persecution from without, concluded, "For to me, to live is Christ, and to die is gain" (Philippians 1:21).

Character Changes Through the Dark Night

Saint John of the Cross shares many imperfections that the dark night can purge us of. Here are five of the most common. It is amazing how timely these words, written in the sixteenth century, are to us today.

- *Pride: satisfied with one's own spiritual works, while condemning others who aren't as "mature." Makes light of one's own faults. Feels misunderstood by those who don't see how spiritual they are. Longs to be thought of highly by others.*

- *Anger: Wants everything to go well spiritually. When there is no sweetness in their spiritual walk their natural temper is sour, morose. Angry with others for their faults. Makes self-confident spiritual resolutions and when they fail, are angry at God.*

- *Gluttony: Strives for more and more spiritual experiences. Seeks after feelings in their faith without having real purity. Assumes God is doing nothing if they can't see it. Always searching for feelings and avoids the pain of self-denial.*

- *Envy: Vexed because of other men's goodness—afflicted when others outstrip them on the spiritual road. Don't like to hear others praised. Feels internal pain when not thought of as well as others.*

- *Sloth: Won't do anything in spiritual life that is very hard. If they try it and it doesn't seem right, they won't try again. Seeks to change God's will to fit their own. Feel if they are happy, God is pleased. Measure God by themselves instead of themselves by God.*[14]

My husband and I look back on our two years as missionaries in the Alaskan bush as a crash course in Christian growth. Darkness came unbidden over and over again through persecution, lack of fruit, loneliness, unanswered prayers, unfulfilled dreams, and senseless tragedy. One experience in particular changed us forever.

Shortly after we arrived in our small village, a missionary from another village came to visit. We were so excited to meet another believer. Our excitement withered as he informed us that we were liberals and that he would fight any work we tried to establish. For the next year we tried to love him—

attending his services, encouraging the few believers to support his ministry, and praying for God to bless Him.

One night at a service of five people (including us), this man demanded that the other three choose between him and us. We were heartbroken— not just at our own pain, but at the devastation this could bring to young converts. We wept that night. I wanted to go home, give up, and let the other missionary do his job.

Pouring out our hearts before God, we asked *why*, pleading for peace. In the morning, only one thing was clear; we had to do what God called us to do. He brought us there—He would sustain us. For the next year we clutched God's call on our lives like drowning swimmers holding a lifeline. This was all we had. Every other reason for being there slowly disintegrated before our eyes.

The growth we gained through that has never left. In ministry after ministry since, we've found that while others may question or criticize, the work may bear little fruit, painful circumstances may be thrust upon us, God has called us. This kind of peace is birthed in the trenches of battle through the long dark night.

John of the Cross tells us the dark night will produce a spiritual soberness as our desires are curbed and our needs lessened. The unfairness and inequities of life do not easily rile, the rejection of others does not threaten, and the confusion of life without answers does not destroy. We have learned to rest in the arms of God, who holds all things together by His power. It is enough.

The Dark Night's Promise

We may not know what God is doing in the deserts, darkness, and deaths of our particular dark nights. But we can be assured of this: He is at work, doing something incredible and life-changing.

Madame Guyon summarized her seven-year dark night this way: "I was inexpressibly overjoyed to find Him, whom I thought I had lost forever, returned to me again with unspeakable magnificence and purity . . . all I had enjoyed before was only a peace, a gift of God, but now I received and possessed the God of peace."[15]

Where are you in your spiritual walk right now? Facing the darkness? Sensing some dryness? Wandering without answers? God stands before you today with words of comfort and hope:

> Do not call to mind the former things, or ponder things of the past. Behold, I will do something new, now it will spring forth; will you not be aware of it? I will even make a roadway in the wilderness, rivers in the desert (Isaiah 43:18–19).

Cling to Him, to His promise, to His own crucifixion and resurrection as you learn of Prayer Through the Dark Night.

Practicing Prayer: To What Will You Cling?

Heart Preparation

Slowly read Isaiah 43:18–20. Read it aloud again, personalizing it, hearing the voice of God speak it to you today. Sit quietly, contemplating all that He might want to do through the dark nights you have encountered or will face. Thank Him for the "something new" He promises.

Read Habakkuk 3:17–19. In your own prayer journal, write a prayer with this as your model. List the things you fear, the things that would destroy your hope, the things that may never come to be in your spiritual life. Finish it as Habakkuk did: Yet I will exult . . .

Commit to reading through this prayer several times over the next few weeks.

Moving Forward

The dark night connects us with God in ways hard to describe. Like a distant foreign land, unless you travel there yourself, you will never comprehend the unique sights and sounds it offers. The treasures found in the dark night find root deep within the cavern of our blossoming soul.

As we go forward, we will learn how to embrace the Lover of our soul more fully, resting beneath His sheltering wings. There is no greater joy in our faith. Love for God settles into our very pores. No matter what happens, we love Him, and long to show our love. Through Contemplative Prayer, we will explore the kind of intimacy with Christ that finds expression in breathtaking silence and whispers of adoration.

Notes

1. Robert Nash, *The Nun at Her Pri-Dieu* (Maryland: Newman Press, 1950), p. 83.
2. Brennan, Manning, *The Signature of Jesus on the Pages of Our Lives* (Sisters, Ore.: Multnomah Press, 1992), p. 122.
3. Jeanne Guyon, *Madame Guyon: An Autobiography* (Chicago: Moody Press), pp. 157–158.
4. Manning, p. 122.
5. Francois Fenelon, *Christian Perfection* (New York: Harper and Row, 1947), p. 171.
6. Guyon, p. 194.
7. Richard Foster, *Prayer, Finding the Heart's True Home* (San Francisco: Harper-SanFrancisco, 1992), p. 22.
8. Nash, p. 197.
9. Manning, p. 110.
10. Hannah Hurnard, *Hinds Feet on High Places* (Wheaton: Tyndale House Publishers, 1977), pp. 172–173.
11. Hurnard, p. 176.
12. John of the Cross, *The Dark Night of the Soul* (Greenwood, S.C.: The Attic Press, 1973), p. 55.

13. Oswald Chambers, *My Utmost for His Highest* (New York: Dodd, Mead & Co.), p. 285.
14. John of the Cross, p. 48.
15. Guyon, p. 191.

CHAPTER EIGHT

CONTEMPLATIVE PRAYER

Let me sing the song of Love, let me follow Thee, my Beloved on high, let my soul spend itself in Thy praise, rejoicing through Love. Let me love Thee more than myself, nor love myself but for Thee.
Thomas à Kempis

Some experiences write themselves on our memory with such force that we never lose the sense of them. This happened to me as a nineteen-year-old college student—disillusioned about my future and distant from God. An elderly aunt took me under her wings, filling my life with the comfort of her stable presence.

One day we stood at a gas station waiting for our car to be filled. It was a mundane task on an ordinary day, until she spoke the words that brought the Spirit of God crashing into the walls of my heart: "Honey, you just need to fall in love with Jesus Christ."

I was stunned. The words doused me like a spring rain, filling my mind and heart and the air that I breathed. That day my true love affair with the Maker of the universe was birthed. Today I love Him in ways I never dreamed, and my capacity to love Him more is like a well that cannot run dry.

What does this have to do with Contemplative Prayer? Contemplation is the expression of a pure and passionate love affair between you and God. It is supernatural intimacy that is difficult to describe. "Can an earthly lover describe in words what occurs in his heart when his beloved is near? Could he if he tried? And would he even want to tell you? In the soul's most delicate communions, there is light and love beyond telling. . . ."[1]

In many ways the journey on which this book has led you finds its destination here in Contemplative Prayer. Yet it is a journey that never ends, a destination to which we never fully arrive. We have just stepped over the border into a new country.

Contemplative Prayer leads us to places we've not known, to a Savior whom we've clung to at a distance. When we taste of the fruit of the land, we know we are on holy ground. We meet our Redeemer in fresh and wondrous ways. We take God's fiery love into the bosom of our souls. We give back selfless adoration.

Contemplation is private, personal, and heart-wrenching. We cannot learn it from someone else. We cannot experience it through greater knowledge. We cannot live it in continual activity. We cannot practice it without passionate desire. We must continue the journey—one step at a time—into the mystical, all-absorbing love of our eternal Lover.

DAY ONE: AM I READY?

It is not uncommon for those who have lived a life of contemplation to caution the rest of us about rushing into it. Contemplative Prayer is a precious part of growing in Christ, but if one isn't ready, he may suffer like a young child given meat that his fragile system cannot yet digest.

This section is not to discourage you from all God offers, but to provide some guidelines to make this prayer experience one of glory to God and growth for you.

The most important prerequisite to Contemplative Prayer is your level of commitment to obedience. Ask yourself these questions:

- Am I giving control of my life to God on a regular basis?

- When I look back at my spiritual life, do I see a consistent pattern of growing obedience?
- Are there things God controls in my life now, which I held to myself in the past?
- Is every area of my life, as far as I can see, open to the purifying fire of God's conviction and molding?
- Is it my heart's desire to belong completely and wholly to Him?

If you answer yes to these questions, your heart may be ready for Contemplative Prayer. Richard Foster offers several other indicators: a hunger for intimacy with God, the ability to forgive others at great personal cost, the living sense that God alone can satisfy the longings of the human heart, deep satisfaction in prayer, a realistic assessment of your own strengths and weaknesses, freedom from pride about your spirituality, and a demonstrated ability to live life patiently and wisely.[2]

The longing for God that draws us into Contemplative Prayer is not feeling-based. It transcends emotional fervor or experiential joy. Our desire to be with Him is so fierce that everything else seems bland to our spiritual taste buds.

When we have moved beyond the need for gifts to the adoration of the Giver, we are ready for Contemplative Prayer. When inexplicable circumstances or piercing questions of faith don't shake our walk with Him, we are ready for Contemplative Prayer. When we know without any doubt that we could never leave Him, we are ready for Contemplative Prayer.

Contemplative Prayer penetrates our heart of hearts, probing the deepest rooms of our interior soul. It leaves no stone unturned, no darkness unlit. God's love burns to our very core. It is wonderful and painful and through it He changes us into His likeness.

It is no shame to be unprepared for Contemplative Prayer. God loves each of His children and longs to reveal as much of himself as we can receive.

If you aren't ready, set your heart toward seeking Him in other ways. Return to other chapters of this book, practicing their truths until they have become second nature to you.

If you believe you may be ready, humble yourself before God. (If you feel confident because of your spirituality or natural ability, ask God to strip you of these dependencies.) When you are broken before Him, you can go forward into contemplation.

The following exercise is crucial to your understanding of Contemplative Prayer. Please spend plenty of time on it, opening your heart to God's gentle probing. This is so very private, so very personal a matter, that you must bring it to Jesus—He alone can show you.

Preparing for Contemplative Prayer— Looking Back

This book has led you on a journey into various ways to relate to our Father. Evaluate your walk with Christ in light of each chapter through the following questions. This will help you in your decision concerning Contemplative Prayer.

The Journey Begins: *Is my discipline of prayer well-established? Do I regularly and consistently spend time in prayer with God, for the purpose of getting to know Him more?*

Meditative Prayer: *Has the Word become a natural part of my prayer time? Do I bring my mind, heart, and will to the verses I read in His presence? Has biblical truth taken root in me on a consistent basis through my prayer life?*

Scripture Praying: *Do the pages of the Bible spring to life in my prayer time? Have I experienced the sense of God's presence through the events I read there? Am I regularly getting to know Him more through prayerful visualization of His Word?*

Listening Prayer: *Have I learned to be still in His Presence? Is God's voice familiar to me? Do I daily open myself, listening for God's personal word? Do I*

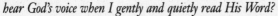

hear God's voice when I gently and quietly read His Word?

Recollective Prayer: *Have I learned to bring all the parts of my life to God regularly for evaluation and reflection? Do I recognize His hand in the events of my life? Do I lean on Him for future guidance?*

Prayer of Detachment: *Am I loving the world less and Christ more as I get to know Him? Can I point to specific areas of attachment to the world that I have let go of? Do I consistently seek God's face and eternal perspective in the way I live my life?*

Prayer Through the Dark Night: *Have I learned the secret of faith when things seem dry, dark, or desperate? Do I know that I can trust Him even when I don't understand His purposes? Do I love God for himself alone? Am I willing to lose everything so that I may know Him?*

Practicing Prayer: Seek the Lord

Heart Preparation

Acclimate yourself to God's presence. Be still and quiet before Him for a few minutes, meditating on Jeremiah 31:3. Confess your fears, weaknesses, and sins in light of His love. Commit to complete honesty as you come before Him today.

Look through the chart: *Preparing for Contemplative Prayer—Looking Back*. With a piece of paper in hand (or perhaps your prayer journal), work through the questions for each chapter. Answer them honestly and openly.

When you have finished, look back at your answers. Bring them before God, praying for His divine guidance and instruction. Pray through these questions:

- Is there some area of prayer I need to spend more time on before going forward? If so, which?
- Do I see a weakness I need to work on—such as discipline, commitment to God's Word, willingness to be changed?
- Recognizing that the prayer journey is a process—do I feel my efforts to know God are consistent and heartfelt?
- Have I reached a place in my walk with God where knowing Him is the continual, active desire of my heart? Does my life demonstrate this or is it something I just say?

After you have prayed through these questions, form a plan for future prayer times. Write down which chapters you would like to return to for a while. Keep in mind that each of these tools weaves together the tapestry of our inner prayer journey, yet our goal is for them to become such a part of us that we practice them freely.

Finally, seek God's clear guidance concerning moving forward in this chapter. If you aren't ready, thank Him for what is to come. If you feel you are, offer yourself to Him for all He wants to do.

DAY TWO: PREPARATION

A new art form swept across the world in the early 1990s, taking captive the imaginations of children and adults alike. Called *Magic Eye* pictures, artists arranged computer generated dots to create one image to the naked eye, but a completely different 3-D picture just beyond the obvious. For example, one very popular illustration portrayed dozens of red roses in rows. Through discipline and skill, beneath the rose picture, one could observe a large three-dimensional heart.

After several months of trying, I finally found success with the *Magic Eye* book my son got for Christmas. The trick was to look very hard at what lay

just beyond the surface. I had to train my eyes to stare into the depths, letting go of the images in front of me. When I did, a brand new picture emerged. But, the second I got distracted by the page itself, I would lose the image.

Contemplative Prayer is a lot like that. We train our spiritual eyes to look past all that surrounds and distracts, until the image of God himself transfixes us. (This is not a physical vision, but a spiritual one.) At first, we may only get a glimpse before we are distracted again. But through practice, we encounter Him more swiftly, holding the vision longer.

Contemplate:

The act of looking attentively at something[3]

So how do we train ourselves in contemplation? This kind of prayer is not easily dissected into steps and procedures. I feel completely at a loss trying to write about it, but I can share some things that will help lead you to the water's edge. Like teaching someone to swim—you will have to get in the water to really learn. Four things can prepare you to dive into the deep end of Contemplative Prayer: protect your mind, purify your heart, praise your Redeemer, and present yourself to God.

Protect Your Mind

While Contemplative Prayer clears our mind of worldly thoughts and distractions, we want to take care that we don't leave it vulnerable to Satan's attacks. He is always sending lies to keep us from God's protective embrace. Giving in to these lies unleashes demonic activity and wages war within our mind.

First, we must be grounded in God's Word in every form of prayer we undertake. The Word alone has the power to transform our minds into godliness. I almost always begin my time of contemplation reading aloud from the Psalms or other portions of God's Word.

Second, we affirm our commitment to Jesus Christ and His will for our time together. We state our intention to give the Holy Spirit full control, and we acknowledge His presence. Our heart asserts allegiance to the living God—no other influences are welcome in our time of Contemplative Prayer.

A great way to combine both steps is to work through Ephesians 6:11–18, making sure every piece of our spiritual armor is in place. At first, preparing our minds may take some time and concentration, until it becomes the habit of our devotional life.

Purify Your Heart

Listen—this very moment Jesus speaks, and the earth shakes: "Blessed are the pure in heart, for they shall see God" (Matthew 5:8). Did you hear that? "They shall *see* God." Do you long to see God? Purity is the only prerequisite. David said, "Who may ascend into the hill of the LORD? And who may stand in His holy place? He who has clean hands and a pure heart" (Psalm 24:3–4).

A pure heart lets go of all other affections and desires. It struggles to seek God and God alone. The fire of God's holiness consumes it, and nothing else matters but to do His will. An anonymous author from the fourteenth century put it this way:

> One thing I tell you, He is a jealous lover and will permit no fellowship and will not kindle your desire unless He alone can work within your will. He asks no other help than your own willingness.

He wills that you but gaze upon Him and abandon yourself to Him.[4]

We are a tabernacle in which God himself dwells. As we empty each room of the grime and clutter, He fills it with the light of His presence. To see God, we simply clean house—daily, moment by moment, and consistently as we come in prayer before Him.

Praise Your Redeemer

Adoration is the cornerstone for true Contemplative Prayer. Our passionate love for Christ shoots up like a fountain in streams of praise for all He is. We don't exude empty emotionalism, but our hearts overflow with deep gratitude for this Lover we have come to know.

Paul Billheimer aptly reminds us that, "Adoration decentralizes self and demands a shift of center from self to God."[5]

We may begin with praise and thanksgiving for all God has done for us. We consider the cross; looking carefully at the freedom it bought us. We hold Christ's sufferings close, seeing His agony, reflecting on our unworthiness—contemplating what our life would be like without Him.

At some point in our eagerness to exalt Him, His love carries us away. What He has done folds into the fabric of who He is. The very nature of God grips us—we comprehend that not only does he love us perfectly, but He *is* perfect love. We can only adore Him.

Present Yourself to God

Finally, in preparation for Contemplative Prayer, we present ourselves quietly to God. Like a bride entering her wedding chamber, we offer our pure, expectant love. We turn our hearts inward to the living Lover of our souls, allowing nothing else to pull us away from His embrace.

We remain still, gently releasing any need to speak or act. A hush settles as we wait upon God. We listen, not so much for words, but for a holy sense of God's closeness to cover us. Caught up in love, we are ready for Contemplative Prayer.

Practicing Prayer: Prepare Your Soul

Heart Preparation

Protect Your Mind: Read the following affirmations based on Ephesians 6:11–18:

- I am protected by the full armor of God—Satan's schemes have no power over me.
- I am protected by God's truth.
- I am protected by the righteousness of Jesus Christ himself.
- I am protected by the Gospel of God's peace.
- I am protected by my faith in God from all lies of the evil one.
- I am redeemed by the blood of Jesus Christ.
- I hold in my hand the Word of God to pierce the darkness and radiate God's light.
- The living Christ alone has access to my mind and heart this day.

Purify Your Heart: Take some time to isolate the motives and intentions of your heart. Let go of any desire other than to see God as He is. Invite God to walk with you through the rooms of your heart. Allow His gentle Spirit to purify and enlighten as you go.

Praise Your Redeemer: Read Isaiah 61:1–3 quietly. Write the verses in your prayer journal as if God had just spoken these truths to you personally. Read what you have written aloud, thanking God for each specific thing He holds out. Reflect on each part of the promise. Worship quietly with words of adoration for all God is, based on these verses.

Present Yourself to God: Be very still and quiet. Gently turn inward to the indwelling Christ. Silently yield yourself to Him. Be still. Allow the hush of His presence to permeate your mind and heart. Repeat the following verse a few times: "Whom have I in heaven but thee? And besides Thee, I desire nothing on earth" (Psalm 73:25).

DAY THREE: THE FACE OF GOD

When I first fell in love with my husband, I knew nothing could be more wonderful. Looking back twenty-one years later, I realize our young love was a mixture of giddy crushes, raging hormones, and blissful naiveté. The wonderful thing about marriage and many years together is the varied faces love comes to wear.

There is the gentle, quiet love where we enjoy hours together without words, and the familiar love that shows up in knowing glances and winks across the room. We know a lighthearted love that lets us laugh together even in the midst of pain. Physical passion now encompasses our bodies, minds, and souls—this too is a face of love.

God's love is also multifaceted. He is a shepherd, tenderly holding us when we've fallen, and a father running toward us as we cautiously come home. He is a mother hen, weeping over our neediness, and a hurting friend longing for our loyalty.

In Contemplative Prayer, we encounter Him, comprehending nuances of His love in fresh ways. We hold those moments of revelation, living in their warmth and light, experiencing firsthand God's compassion. We are lost in it, unable to do anything but love Him back. We say little—our minds stilled in the wonder of intimacy.

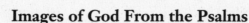
Images of God From the Psalms

A shield—Psalm 3:3

My hiding place—Psalm 32:7

Sustainer of my soul—Psalm 54:4

Rock of habitation—Psalm 71:3

God who works wonders—Psalm 77:14

Holy and awesome—Psalm 111:9

My fortress—Psalm 18:2

Mighty One—Psalm 45:3

Father of the fatherless—Psalm 68:5

Strength of my heart—Psalm 73:26

Avenger of evil—Psalm 99:8

Maker of heaven and earth—Psalm 115:15

The How-to of Intimacy

The Bible overflows with the facets of God's love, but we limit our experience to familiar themes. Then—as ridiculous as it seems—we get bored with God. Contemplative Prayer broadens our basis for loving God and opens our hearts to ever-growing intimacy with our Creator and Redeemer.

First, consider which face of God you want to know more. (See Charts: *Images of God From the Psalms* and *Pictures of Jesus*.) Read His words slowly, letting the thoughts sink in. Ponder their meaning and personalize their message.

Place yourself right in the middle of the picture. For example, if He is your shelter, feel the storms of life crashing around you. Envision the things that disturb your peace. See God surrounding you, holding out His massive hands so that nothing touches you. Wait before Him, holding the sense of His presence.

Love Him Back

At some point, you will want to respond. Pour out your love to Him. Speak very little—perhaps a phrase of adoration such as *I love you, Lord*—repeating it two or three times. Enter into intimacy with Him.

Thomas Merton calls this a *Contemplative Gaze*. "Knowing by faith that He is present with you . . . relax in a simple contemplative gaze that keeps your attention peacefully aware of Him hidden somewhere in this deep cloud into which you also feel yourself drawn to enter."[6]

Pictures of Jesus From the New Testament

The Good Shepherd—John 10:1–16

Rejected by men—Luke 4:29; 17:25

Silent when accused—Matthew 26: 62, 63

Great Intercessor—John 17:1–26

The Consoler—John 14:1–3

The Servant—John 13:1–10

The Great Physician—John 5:1–9

The Water of Life—John 7:37

The Bread of Life—John 6:32–58

The Alpha and the Omega— Revelation 1:8

The Lamb—Revelation 17:14

King of Kings—Revelation 19:16

The Lion of the Tribe of Judah— Revelation 5:5

This may last a few minutes or an hour. Priests who live a cloistered life spend hours or days contemplating one facet of God's love. While most of us do not share their calling, we can learn from their discipline. Intimacy takes time. The deeper we desire our love affair with God to be, the more time we must spend in quietness and adoration before Him.

Contemplative Prayer has the capacity to impact our spiritual life in ways we can't imagine. All the frustrated longings of our soul are met in those moments of quiet attentiveness before Him. Mother Teresa has said the most perfect prayer she prays is this: *I look upon Him, He looks upon me*. Contemplation is pure love—poured out upon us by the Lover of our souls and offered back to Him in genuine humility.

Practicing Prayer: I Look at Him—He Looks at Me

Heart Preparation

Protect Your Mind: Read Psalm 113 aloud, personalizing it, affirming its truth for this day.

Purify Your Heart: Quietly open the rooms of your heart—offering everything that comes to your mind to God. Repent, if necessary, resting in His strength to change.

Praise Your Redeemer: Sing a couple of praise choruses or hymns of praise softly to the Lord.

Present Yourself to God: Breathe deeply, allowing all distractions to fade away. Set your mind and heart on God, quieting every thought. Gently remind yourself that God is here, ready to meet you, to love you, and to reveal more of himself.

Read Isaiah 25:6–9. Envision a beautiful banquet where you are given the seat of honor. See Jesus coming to serve you. What does He offer? Read the passage again slowly. Spend some time receiving the salvation Jesus offers at this banquet table. Then humble your heart—pour out your gratitude for having been invited at all.

Sit quietly in the warmth of His love, the security of His presence. Do not rush. Listen, in case He wants to speak to you.

When your time of contemplation is finished, write a response in your prayer journal.

DAY FOUR: SILENCE IN CONTEMPLATIVE PRAYER

Silence is perhaps the most difficult discipline for evangelical Christians. We've heard little teaching on the subject and are woefully short on mentors. In the Catholic Church, many ministers (priests and nuns) devote their entire life to contemplation and monastic living. The rest of us can learn from them how to incorporate silent contemplation into our own busy lives. We have no such tradition to glean from.

Yet the very holiness of God demands silence. "Be silent, all flesh, before the LORD; for He is aroused from His holy habitation" (Zechariah 2:13).

"But the LORD is in His holy temple. Let all the earth be silent before Him" (Habakkuk 2:20).

The literal translation of this verse is *hush before Him, all the earth*. It's almost as if when we encounter the living God, the only appropriate response is silent adoration.

Our love affair with Christ sooner or later brings us to a point where all we want to do is look at His face, helpless to say anything. "My soul waits in silence for God only" (Psalm 62:1).

We wait in silence as we contemplate God who is Love. We seek His face, stripped of the masks of wordiness. In gazing at Him, we see our own need, our desperate sinfulness. We repent, bathed in His tears of compassion. Our tender Lover pours the oil of His Spirit into the gaping wounds of our humanity. We are healed. We long to love Him back.

God assures us that in eternity He will first personally wipe every tear from our eyes, removing any vestige of sadness we have known on earth. But then what? Consider this dramatic development: "And when He broke the seventh seal, there was silence in heaven for about half an hour" (Revelation 8:1).

All creation will be so taken aback at the presence of God that we will in a sense be struck dumb. And if a day is as a thousand years to God, we will stay mute for twenty-one years! Contemplative Prayer is simply a taste of eternity.

An ancient saint, Gregory of Nyssa, wrote: "The time to be silent is when we seek to tell of the essence of God instead of what He has done . . . human speech finds it impossible to express that reality which transcends all thought and every concept."[7]

John Bisagno calls this an "exercise that demands our keenest attention, our most alert frame of mind, and all of our soul's attention to the heavenly Voice."[8]

Dick Eastman deems it "the act of soul surrender."[9]

Another author agrees: "We do not speak. He speaks. We do not ask. He asks. He is the music that fills the universe and we—we with our first fumbling steps—now catch the rhythm of the dance."[10]

There is no Contemplative Prayer without silence and there is no silence without fervent discipline. Silence before God goes against everything in our natural selves. In stillness we become vulnerable, alone with the Creator of the Universe who knows our deepest thoughts, hidden longings, and shameful secrets.

Silent contemplation before God is both painful and powerful. In pain we are purified. Listen to the cry of John of the Cross:

> O living flame of love
> That tenderly wounds my soul
> In its deepest center!
> Since
> Now You are not oppressive,
> Now Consummate! If it be Your will:
> Tear through the veil of this sweet encounter![11]

God gently consumes the rank residue of rebellion within our hearts, and then speaks something fresh to our souls.

Recently a friend of mine shared how the woman with the alabaster bottle (Luke 7:36–38) had touched her heart. She told me: "I want to be the kind of woman who wastes herself on Jesus. I want to wile away my time in His presence. I want to squander my possessions for His glory. I want to expend everything that is dear to me, that I might in some small measure, give Him back the love He's given me."

This is Contemplative Prayer—wasting ourselves on God. In extravagance of soul we seek His face. In generosity of heart, we glean His gentle touch. In excessiveness of spirit, we love Him and His love comes back to us a hundredfold.

Silence is the wing by which Contemplative Prayer flies to the feet of the living God. There we wait, for our hope is from Him (Psalm 62:5). Time is the only price we pay for this ecstatic encounter with Holiness. It costs us nothing but our all to love and be loved by Him.

Practicing Prayer: Wasting Ourselves on God

Heart Preparation

Protect Your Mind: Read 1 Peter 2:9–10 aloud. Read it again putting your name in it: (e.g. *For I, John, am a chosen race; I, John, am a royal priest*, etc.) Affirm these truths for your time today.

Purify Your Heart: Quietly open the rooms of your heart—go deeper than before, letting God reveal attitudes, anxieties, or needs you rarely acknowledge. Repent, if necessary, resting in His strength to change.

Praise Your Redeemer: Choose an attribute of God. (See Psalm 145 for ideas.) First begin to thank Him for specific things this attribute gives you. Then worship Him because He is the essence of this attribute.

Present Yourself to God: Breathe deeply, allowing all distractions to fade away. Set your mind and heart on God, quieting every thought. Gently affirm that God is present.

Read Luke 7:36–47. Think of this woman. Try to feel the love for Christ that compelled her to act as she did. See yourself pouring out this kind of love to Jesus. Spend some time meditating on these acts, personalizing them as you contemplate the One who forgave you so much.

- She risked everything to be with Him.
- She gave her most valuable possession—poured it out on Him.
- She wept, washing His feet with her tears, drying them with her hair.
- She kissed His feet, anointing them with perfume.

Be still and quiet in love and adoration for Jesus, your Redeemer. Remain in this state for an extended period of time, bringing your heart to Him with occasional, simple words of adoration.

DAY FIVE: LOVING GOD

Listen! My beloved! Behold, he is coming, climbing on the mountains, leaping on the hills! . . . Behold, he is standing behind our wall, he is looking through the windows, he is peering through the lattice. My beloved responded and said to me, "Arise, my darling, my beautiful one, and come along. . . . O my dove, in the clefts of the rock, in the secret place of the steep pathway, let me see your form, let me hear your voice; for your voice is sweet, and your form is lovely" (Song of Solomon 2:8–10, 14).

Jesus calls to you—like a lover looking through the window at His beloved one, He watches your life, aching for you to come along. Will you? Will you run to the secret place with Him? This is Contemplative Prayer's mystical beckoning. In gentleness He cradles you in His arms and you belong to Him alone.

This is a private part of the journey—no one else can go along. But many have journeyed before us and their words are like road signs pointing the way. This next section will pull back the curtain on the deep intimacy other saints have known with Jesus. Perhaps their voices will tug at your own heartstrings. Ponder each reading before moving to the next.

Brennan Manning, at one time a Catholic priest, tells of his seven-month retreat into solitude, living in a cave in Spain. He saw no one and endured very primitive living conditions. In one side of the cave a three-foot crucifix hung on the wall. Every night at 2:00 A.M. he knelt in contemplation before it for one hour. One night in particular, the love of God broke through his humanity. He reflects:

> I looked at the crucifix for a long time, figuratively saw the blood streaming from every pore of His body and heard the cry of His wounds: *This isn't a joke. It is not a laughing matter to Me that I have loved you.* The longer I looked the more I realized that no man has ever loved me and no one ever could love me as He did. I went out of the cave, stood on the precipice, and shouted into the darkness, "Jesus, are you crazy? Are you out of your mind to have loved me so much?"[12]

Ponder quietly what others have said, pausing to reflect after each one.

> The interior life is like a sea of love in which the soul is plunged and is, as it were, drowned in love. Just as a mother holds her child's face in her hands to cover it with kisses, so does God hold the devout man.[13]

John Vianney

The infinite sanctity of God seeks the love of a sinful creature and, in order to win it, lifts the soul and shares with it His own very life. . . . Admittedly, there is a mystery in all this. Why such a God should love such a creature, and in such a manner, baffles the powers of our intelligence.[14]

Robert Nash

Contemplation is nothing else but a secret, peaceful, and loving infusion of God, which, if admitted, will set the soul on fire with the spirit of love.[15]

John of the Cross

Nothing was more easy to me than prayer. . . . The taste of God was so great, so pure, unblended and uninterrupted, that it drew and absorbed the power of my soul into a profound recollection without act or discourse. I had now no sight but of Jesus Christ alone.[16]

Madame Guyon

Although it be good to think upon the kindness of God, and to love Him and praise Him for it; yet it is far better to gaze upon the pure essence of Him and to love Him and praise Him for himself.[17]

Anonymous

Usually prayer is a question of groaning rather than speaking, tears rather than words.[18]

Saint Augustine

Prayer is a response to the outpouring love and concern with which God lays siege to every soul. When that reply to God is most direct of all, it is called adoration. Adoration is *loving back*. . . . In adoration we enjoy God. We ask nothing except to be near Him. We want nothing except that we would like to give Him all. Out of this kind of prayer comes the cry Holy! Holy! Holy! In the school of adoration the soul learns why the approach to every goal had left it restless.[19]

Douglas Steere

There are many heads resting on Christ's bosom, but there's room for yours there.[20]

Samuel Rutherford

I still think the prayer without words is the best—if one can really achieve it. . . . When the golden moments come, when God enables one really to pray without words, who but a fool would reject the gift?[21]

C. S. Lewis

I don't say anything to God. I just sit and look at Him and let Him look at me.[22]

Old Peasant of Ars

Ask yourself: *Am I down in the flaming center of God? Have I come into the deeps, where the soul meets with God and knows His love and power? Have I discovered God as a living Immediacy, a sweet Presence stirring life-renovating Power within me?*[23]

Thomas Kelly

This is an exalted and imperceptible prayer; for the whole reason why we pray is to be united into the vision and contemplation of Him to whom we pray, wonderfully rejoicing with reverent fear, and with so much sweetness and delight in Him that we cannot pray at all except as He moves us at the time.[24]

Julian of Norwich

And when God reveals himself to us in contemplation we must accept Him as He comes to us, in His own obscurity, in His own silence, not interrupting Him with arguments or words, conceptions or activities that belong to the level of our own tedious and labored existence.[25]

Thomas Merton

O my God, O love, love thyself in me! . . . I only want to live to be consumed before thee, as a lamp burns ceaselessly before thine altars. I do not exist for myself at all. . . . Love on, O love! Love in thy weak creature! Love thy supreme beauty! O beauty, O infinite goodness, O infinite love: burn, consume, transport, annihilate my heart, make it a perfect holocaust![26]

Francois Fenelon

Our God is there, just there, cherishing you, desiring me, coaxing and beguiling us, until we are simply drunk with his closeness and love.[27]

Emilie Griffin

Sometimes you want to talk to your son, and sometimes you want to hold him tight in silence. God is that way with us; He wants to hold still with us in silence.[28]

Frank Laubauch

So wait before the Lord. Wait in the stillness. And in that stillness, assurance will come to you. You will know that you are heard; you will know that your Lord ponders the voice of your humble desires; you will hear quiet words spoken to you yourself, perhaps to your grateful surprise and refreshment.[29]

Amy Carmichael

What we need most in order to make progress is to be silent before this great God with our appetites and our tongue, for the language He best hears is silent love.[30]

Sister Eileen Lyddon

Unless a person is acquainted with trembling awe, reaching down to the very ground of his being, at the thought of God's nature ... he will not be ready for the contemplation of Jesus Christ.[31]

Hans Urs Von Balthasar

Jesus is always waiting for us in silence. In this silence He listens to us; it is there that He speaks to our souls. And there, we hear His voice.... In this silence we find a new energy and a real unity.... There is unity of our thoughts with His thoughts, unity of our prayers with His prayers, unity of our actions with His actions, of our life with His life.[32]

Mother Teresa

Jesus, lover of my soul,
Let me to Thy bosom fly.

Charles Wesley

Practicing Prayer: Your Own Love Affair

Heart Preparation
Protect Your Mind: Read Psalm 91 aloud, personalizing it, affirming its truth for this day.

Purify Your Heart: Quietly open the rooms of your heart—offering everything that comes to your mind to God. Ask His Spirit to visit every room of your heart, illuminating the dusty corners with His light. Let His love cleanse you.

Praise Your Redeemer: Tell God at least ten things about Him that bring you joy. Write them in your prayer journal.

Present Yourself to God: Breathe deeply, allowing all distractions to fade away. Set your mind and heart on God, quieting every thought. See yourself as pure and holy, entering the bridal chamber to give your love and receive His. Gently remind yourself that God is here, ready to love and be loved by you.

Sit quietly before the Lord, absorbing His presence. Allow images to pass through your spirit—of Jesus' ministry on earth, the cross, etc. As each one comes, reflect on it and worship Him silently. (If this is difficult, read the account of the crucifixion from one of the Gospels.)

Remain in stillness and silence before Him for an extended period of time. Do not speak, other than to gently say: *I love you, Lord; I adore you,* etc. Let your heart commune with His. Listen carefully as you wait on Him. Reflect on the impressions of your heart. Wait on the Lord. Love Him. Receive His love.

When you are finished, write a response in your prayer journal.

Moving Forward

We began our inner prayer journey with the words: *Behold, now begins an eternal craving and insatiable longing,* which were written in the thirteenth century by a contemplative. Having lived as a hermit and monastic, this man understood the deeper life of prayer. With poignancy he reflects:

"The inward stirring and touching of God makes us hungry and yearning; for the Spirit of God hunts our spirit; and the more He touches it, the greater our hunger and our craving. And this is the life of love in its highest working. . . ."[33]

The Spirit of God hunts your spirit. As you respond, He stirs within you more desire for Him. It is a beautiful, unending cycle of love with the Maker of your soul. The journey has truly just begun. I pray you will grow in the grace of knowing, loving, and being loved by the Eternal Lover, our Lord Jesus Christ. To Him be glory forever.

Notes

1. As quoted in David Hazard, *You Set My Spirit Free—A 40-Day Journey in the Company of John of the Cross* (Minneapolis: Bethany House Publishers, 1994), p. 99.

2. Richard Foster, *Prayer: Finding the Heart's True Home* (San Francisco: HarperSanFrancisco, 1992), p. 156.

3. *The New Lexicon Webster's Dictionary of the English Language* (New York: Lexicon Publications, Inc.) p. 210

4. Anonymous, *The Cloud of Unknowing* (New York: Harper & Brothers, 1948), p. 10.

5. Paul Billheimer, *Destined for the Throne* (Pennsylvania:Christian Literature Crusade, 1975), p. 118.

6. Thomas Merton, *New Seeds of Contemplation* (New York: Direction Books, 1961), p. 219.

7. Gregory of Nyssa, *From Glory to Glory*, *Selected* and with Introduction by Jean Danielou (New York: Charles Scribner's Sons, 1961), p. 126.

8. John Bisagno, *The Power of Positive Praying* (Grand Rapids: Zondervan, 1965), p. 70.

9. Dick Eastman, *The Hour That Changes the World* (Grand Rapids: Baker Books, 1978), p. 34.

10. Emilie Griffin, *Clinging, The Experience of Prayer* (San Francisco: Harper and Row, 1984), p. 14.

11. John of the Cross, *The Living Flame of Love*, Prologue; stanza 1:1.

12. Brennan Manning, *The Signature of Jesus on the Pages of Our Lives* (Sisters, Ore.: Multnomah Press, 1992), p. 39–40.

13. John Vianney, as quoted in Jill Haak Adels, *The Wisdom of the Saints* (New York: Oxford University Press, 1987), p. 140.

14. Robert Nash, *The Nun at Her Pri-Dieu* (Maryland: Newman Press, 1950), p. 198.

15. Hazard, p. 27.

16. Jeanne Guyon, *Madame Guyon: An Autobiography* (Chicago: Moody Press, undated), p. 76.

17. Anonymous, *Cloud of Unknowing* (New York: Harper & Brothers, 1948), pp. 35–36.

18. Adels, p. 39.

19. Douglas Steere, *Prayer and Worship* (New York: Association Press, 1938), p. 35.

20. Cited by Charles Spurgeon in *My Sermon Notes* (New York: Funk & Wagnalls, undated).

21. C. S. Lewis, *Letters to Malcolm: Chiefly on Prayer* (New York: Harcourt, Brace & World, 1964), p. 11.

22. Adels, p. 37.

23. Thomas Kelly, *The Eternal Promise* (New York: Harper & Row, 1966), p. 21.

24. Julian of Norwich, *Showings* (New York, Paulist Press, 1978), p. 254.

25. Merton, p. 219.

26. Francois Fenelon, *Christian Perfection* (New York: Harper & Row, 1947), p. 135.

27. Griffin, p. 55.

28. Frank C. Laubach, *Letters by a Modern Mystic* (New Jersey: Fleming H. Revell Co., 1937), p. 62.

29. Amy Carmichael, *Thou Gives . . . They Gather* (London: Lutterworth Press, 1959), p. 43.

30. Sister Eileen Lyddon, *Door Through Darkness* (New York: New City Press, 1995), p. 72.

31. Hans Urs Von Balthasar, *Prayer* (San Francisco: Ignatius Press, 1986), p. 159.

32. Mother Teresa, *Total Surrender* (Ann Arbor, Mich.: Servant Publications, 1985), p. 9.

33. Jan Van Ruysbroeck, as quoted in Jill Haak Adels, *The Wisdom of the Saints* (New York: Oxford University Press, 1987), p. 139.

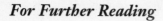

For Further Reading

Celebration of Discipline, Richard Foster (HarperSanFrancisco).
Prayer, Finding the Heart's True Home, Richard Foster (HarperSanFrancisco).
The Cloud of Unknowing, Anonymous (Various publishers).
The Believer's Daily Renewal, Andrew Murray (Bethany House Publishers).
Quiet Talks on Prayer, S. D. Gordon (Revell).
Experiencing the Depths of Jesus Christ, Jeanne Guyon (Various publishers).
The Pursuit of God, A. W. Tozer (Christian Publications).
Making All Things New, Henri Nouwen (HarperSanFrancisco).
Out of Solitude, Henri Nouwen (Ave Maria Press).
Christian Perfection, Francois Fenelon (Bethany House Publishers).
The Hidden Life of Prayer, D. M. M'Intyre (Bethany House Publishers).
Disciplines for the Inner Life, Bob & Michael Benson (Thomas Nelson).
Practicing the Presence of God, Brother Lawrence (Various publishers).
The Spirit of the Disciplines, Dallas Willard (HarperCollins).
The Signature of Jesus on the Pages of Our Lives, Brennan Manning (Multnomah Press).
Madame Guyon: An Autobiography, Jeanne Guyon (Moody Press).
You Set My Spirit Free: A 40-day Journey in the Company of John of the Cross, David Hazard (Bethany House Publishers).
Early Will I Seek Thee: A 40-day Journey in the Company of Augustine, David Hazard (Bethany House Publishers).

Catholic Perspective
Contemplative Prayer, Thomas Merton (Doubleday).
New Seeds of Contemplation, Thomas Merton (New Direction Books).
Confessions, Augustine of Hippo (Various Publishers).
Clinging, the Experience of Prayer, Emilie Griffin (HarperCollins).

The Dark Night of the Soul, John of the Cross (Various publishers).
The Imitation of Christ, Thomas à Kempis (Various publishers).
The Interior Castle, Teresa of Avila (Paulist Press).

Further Information About the Author

For information about Tricia McCary Rhodes' speaking ministry or future books on prayer, please write or call:

New Hope Church
10330 Carmel Mountain Road
San Diego, CA 92129
(619) 538–0888 Ext. 111
(or E-mail: tpraynow@aol.com)